Anonymous

Golden Songs and Ballads for the Children

Anonymous

Golden Songs and Ballads for the Children

ISBN/EAN: 9783744792714

Printed in Europe, USA, Canada, Australia, Japan

Cover: Foto ©Thomas Meinert / pixelio.de

More available books at **www.hansebooks.com**

GOLDEN SONGS

AND

BALLADS

FOR

THE CHILDREN.

SELECTED BY THE AUTHOR OF
"ANNIE'S GOLD CROSS," Etc., Etc.

———◆———

PHILADELPHIA:
PRESBYTERIAN PUBLICATION COMMITTEE,
1334 CHESTNUT STREET.
NEW YORK: A. D. F. RANDOLPH & CO., 770 BROADWAY.

WESTCOTT & THOMSON,
Stereotypers, Philada.

INTRODUCTION.

MANY children and many mothers will thank the lover of poetry whose taste, enthusiasm and labor have been devoted to the preparation of this little volume. In it will be found the cream of many good books compiled for the young, together with other pieces not in those volumes. Few gifts will afford more delight or prove more useful to our dear little boys and girls than our GOLDEN SONGS AND BALLADS. May they carry joy and love into many hearts and enliven many homes!

J. W. D.

GOLDEN SONGS.

—∘∘⟨⟩∘∘—

LITTLE PEOPLE.

A DREARY place would be this earth
 Were there no little people in it;
The song of life would lose its mirth
 Were there no children to begin it!—

No little forms like buds to grow,
 And make admiring hearts surrender;
No little hands on breast and brow
 To keep the thrilling love-chords tender;

No babe within our arms to leap;
 No little feet toward slumber tending;
No little knee in prayer to bend,
 Our lips the sweet words lending.

1 *   5

What would the mothers do for work
  Were there no pants or jackets tearing?
No tiny dresses to embroider?
  No cradle for their watchful caring?

No rosy boys, on wintry morn,
  With satchel to the school-house hasting?
No merry shouts as home they rush,
  No precious morsel for their tasting?

The sterner souls would grow more stern,
  Unfeeling natures more inhuman;
And man to stoic coldness turn,
  And woman would be less a woman.

For in that clime toward which we reach
  Through Time's mysterious dim unfolding,
The little ones with cherub smile
  Are still our Father's face beholding.

So said His voice in whom we trust,
  When in Judea's realms a preacher;
He made a child confront the proud,
  And be, in simple guise, their teacher.

Life's song indeed would lose its charm
   Were there no babies to begin it;
A doleful place this world would be
   Were there no little people in it!

THE PATTER OF LITTLE FEET.

Up with the sun in the morning,
   Away to the garden he hies,
To see if the sleepy blossoms
   Have begun to open their eyes.
Running a race with the wind,
   With a step as light and fleet,
Under my window I hear
   The patter of little feet.

Now to the brook he wanders
   In swift and noiseless flight,
Splashing the sparkling ripples
   Like a fairy water-sprite.
No sand under fabled river
   Has gleams like his golden hair;

No pearly shell is fairer
   Than his slender ankles bare;
Nor the rosiest stem of coral
   That blushes in ocean's bed,
Is sweet as the flush that follows
   Our darling's airy tread.

From a broad window my neighbor
   Looks down on our little cot,
And watches the poor man's blessing:
   I cannot envy his lot.
He has pictures, books and music,
   Bright fountains and noble trees;
Flowers that blossom in vases,
   Birds from beyond the seas;
But never does childish laughter
   His homeward footsteps greet,
His stately halls ne'er echo
   To the tread of innocent feet.
This child is our "speaking picture!"
   A birdling that chatters and sings;
Sometimes a sleeping cherub—
   (Our other one has wings!)

His heart is a charmèd casket,
    Full of all that's cunning and sweet,
And no harpstrings hold such music
    As follows his twinkling feet.

When the glory of sunset opens
    The highway by angels trod,
And seems to unbar the city
    Whose builder and maker is God,
Close to the crystal portal,
    I see by the gates of pearl
The eyes of our other angel,
    A twin-born little girl,

And I ask to be taught and directed
    To guide his footsteps aright,
So that I be accounted worthy
    To walk in sandals of light,
And hear, amid songs of welcome
    From messengers trusty and fleet,
On the starry floor of heaven
    The patter of little feet!

GOD SEES ME.

Through all the busy daylight, through all
    the quiet night,
Whether the stars are in the sky, or the sun
    is shining bright!
In the nursery, in the parlor, in the street,
    or on the stair,
Though I may seem to be alone, yet God is
    always there.
Whatever I may do, wherever I may be,
Although I see him not, yet God sees me.

He knows each word I mean to say before
    the word is spoken,
He knows the thoughts within my heart,
    although I give no token;
When I am naughty, then I grieve my hea-
    venly Father's love,
And every time I really try he helps me
    from above.
Whatever I may do, wherever I may be,
Although I see him not, yet God sees me.

I have kind and tender parents, I have many
    loving friends,
But none love me as God loves me; all that
    is good he sends.
I will walk as God shall lead me, when the
    sun is in the sky,
And lay me down and sleep in peace beneath
    his watchful eye.
Whatever I may do, wherever I may be,
Although I see him not, yet God sees me.

              HYMNS FOR YOUNG CHILDREN.

TREASURE ON EARTH AND TREASURE IN HEAVEN.

BEN ADAM had a golden coin one day,
    Which he put at interest with a Jew:
Year after year, awaiting him it lay
    Until the doubled coin two pieces grew.
And these two, four! so on, till people said,
    "How rich Ben Adam is!" and bowed the
    servile head.

Ben Selim had a golden coin that day,
　　Which to a stranger asking alms he gave,
Who went rejoicing on his unknown way.
　　Ben Selim died, too poor to own a grave ;
But when his soul reached heaven, angels
　　　　with pride
Showed him the wealth to which his coin
　　　　had multiplied.

———◆◇◆———

"PADDLE YOUR OWN CANOE."

Up this world and down this world,
　　And over this world and through,
Though drifted about and tossed without,
　　Still "paddle your own canoe!"

What if breakers rise up ahead,
　　With dark waves rushing through?
Move steadily by, with a steadfast eye,
　　And "paddle your own canoe!"

Never give up when trials come;
　　Never grow sad and blue;

Never sit down with a tear and a frown,
  But "paddle your own canoe!"

Up this world and down this world,
  And over this world and through,
Though weary and worn, bereft and forlorn,
  Still "paddle your own canoe!"

ANNIE E. HONE.

---◆---

LITTLE DICK SNAPPY.

LITTLE Dick Snappy was always unhappy,
  Because he did nothing but fret,
And when he once cried 'twas in vain that
      you tried
  To make him his troubles forget.

His mother once brought him a drum, that
      she bought him
  Hard by at a neighboring fair,
And gave such another to Edward his
      brother,
  And left them their pleasures to share.

2

Little Edward began, like a nice little man,
    To play with his pretty new drum,
But Dick, with a pout, only turned his about
    In his hands, and looked sulky and grum.

"What's the matter, dear Dick? you look
        sad : are you sick ?
Come! march like a soldier with me.
The enemy comes, let us beat on our drums,
    And mamma will our merriment see."

"No, I don't like my toy," said the ill-
        humored boy,
    " And yours is the best and most new;
If you'll give me yours, then I'll go out of
        doors,
    But if not, then I'll kick mine in two."

"Oh no, brother, no! Pray do not say so,
    For a trifle in anger and haste;
Though they're equally new, yet my drum
        I'd give you,
    But I've tied it in knots round my waist."

Then quarrelsome Dick gave his brother a
    kick,
But he did not give him another;
For, saying no more, Edward walked to the
    door,
Only giving one look at his brother.

Then, bursting with spite, with his utmost of
    might
Master Dick trod his drum on the floor;
The parchment did crack; when lo! Edward
    came back,
And his drum in his hands then he bore.

"The string is untied, dearest brother," he
    cried;
"So now I with pleasure will change;"
But when Dick's drum he found lying broke
    on the ground,
Oh how did his countenance change!

"I am really ashamed" (Dick sobbing ex-
    claimed)
   "At the difference between you and me;

But continue my friend and I'll try to amend,
And a good-tempered fellow to be."

FORGIVING.

"And forgive us our trespasses as we forgive them that
trespass against us."

WHEN thou art kneeling down at night
    Beside thy mother's knee to pray,
And thinking over all thy sins
    Done through the busy day,

Then call to mind thy brother's wrong,
    To strife by angry passions driven,
And in thy heart forgive him all,
    As thou wouldst be forgiven.

Go, throw thy little arms around
    His neck, and kiss him tenderly,
Nor turn away with pouting lip
    And sullen, tearful eye.

Thou hast sinned more against thy God
    Than ever brother did to thee;
If he should turn away his face,
    How wretched wouldst thou be!

Dost thou remember, when thy Lord
    Hung on his cruel cross so long,
How in his agony he prayed
    For those who did him wrong?

They nailed his hands, they pierced his feet,
    Their angry hearts no pity knew;
" Father, forgive them," was his cry,
    " They know not what they do."

Go seek thy little brother's side,
    And press to his thy rosy cheek,
And whisper the forgiveness free
    He is too proud to seek.

Then, as the brightest ray from heaven
    Doth on the glittering dewdrop fall,
Thy penitence shall be received,
    And God forgive thee all.
                                MRS. C. F. ALEXANDER.

2 *

ANNA'S GOOD RESOLUTIONS.

Well, now I'll sit down and I'll work very
　　fast,
And try if I can't be a good girl at last;
'Tis better than being so sulky and haughty;
I'm really tired of being so naughty.

For, as dear mamma says, when my work is
　　all done,
There is plenty of time left to play and to
　　run;
But when it is work-time, I ought to sit
　　still;
I know that I ought, and I certainly will.

But for fear, after all, I should get at my
　　play;
I will put little doll in the closet away,
And I'll not look to see what the kitten is
　　doing,
Nor think of a single thing, only my sewing.

I'm sorry I've idled so often before,
But I hope I shall never do so any more;
Mamma will be pleased when she sees how
    I mend—
When I've done this long seam from begin-
    ning to end.

MISS JANE TAYLOR.

POPPiNG CORN.

ONE autumn night, when the wind was high
  And the rain fell in many flashes,
A little boy sat by the kitchen fire,
  A-popping corn in the ashes;
And his sister, a curly-haired child of three,
Sat looking on, just close to his knee.

Pop! pop! and the kernels one by one
  Came out of the embers flying;
The boy held a long pine stick in hand,
  And kept it busily plying;
He stirred the corn, and it snapped the more,
And faster jumped to the clean-swept floor.

Part of the kernels flew one way,
  And a part hopped out the other;
Some flew plump into the sister's lap,
  Some under the stool of the brother;
The little girl gathered them into a heap,
And called them a flock of milk-white sheep.

----o0o----

MORNING HYMN.

THE morning bright, with rosy light,
  Has waked me from my sleep;
Father, I own thy love alone
  Thy little one doth keep.

All through the day, I humbly pray,
  Be thou my Guard and Guide;
My sins forgive and let me live,
  Dear Saviour, near thy side.

Oh make thy rest within my breast,
  Great Spirit of all grace;
Make me like thee—then I shall be
  Prepared to see thy face.

EVENING PRAYER.

Now I lay me down to sleep—
I pray the Lord my soul to keep;
If I should die before I wake,
I pray the Lord my soul to take;
And this I ask for Jesus' sake.

LITTLE MARY.

Before the bright sun rises over the hill,
  In the corn-fields poor Mary is seen,
Impatient her little blue apron to fill
  With the few scattered ears she can glean.

She never looks off nor goes out of her place,
  To play nor to idle nor chat,
Except now and then just to wipe her warm
    face
  And fan herself with her straw hat.

" Why don't you leave off, as others have done,
  And sit with them under the tree?

I fear you will faint in the beams of the sun;
How weary and hot you must be!"

"Oh no, my dear mother lies ill in her bed,
Too feeble to spin or to knit;
My poor little brothers are crying for bread,
And yet we can't give them a bit.

"Then could I be idle, or merry, or play
While they are so hungry and ill?
Ah no! I had rather work hard all the day
My little blue apron to fill."

ON THE LORD'S SIDE.

God's trumpet wakes the slumbering world;
Now each man to his post;
The red-cross banner is unfurled—
Who joins the glorious host?

He who in fealty to the truth,
And counting all the cost,
Doth consecrate his generous youth—
He joins the noble host.

He who, no anger on his tongue
  Nor any idle boast,
Bears steadfast witness against wrong—
  He joins the sacred host.

He who, with calm, undaunted will,
  Ne'er counts the battle lost;
But, though defeated, battles still—
  He joins the faithful host.

He who is ready for the cross,
  The cause despised loves most,
And shuns not pain, or shame, or loss—
  He joins the martyr host.

ROBIN REDBREAST.

COME here, little Robin, and don't be afraid;
  I would not hurt even a feather;
Come here, little Robin, and pick up some
    bread
  To feed you this very cold weather.

Come! come! I won't hurt you, you poor
    little thing!
And pussy-cat is not behind me;
So hop about pretty and put down your wing,
    And pick up the crumbs and don't mind
    me.

Cold winter is come, but it will not last long,
    And summer we soon shall be greeting,
So remember, dear Robin, to sing me a song
    In return for the breakfast you're eating.

WONDERFUL NIGHT!

CHRISTMAS.

WONDERFUL night!
Angels and shining immortals
Thronging thine ebony portals
Fling out their banners of light—
    Wonderful night!

Wonderful night!
Dreamed of by prophets and sages;
Manhood, redeemed for all ages,
Welcomes thy hallowing might,
Wonderful night!

Wonderful night!
Down o'er the stars to restore us,
Leading his flame-winged chorus,
Comes the Eternal to sight—
Wonderful night!

Wonderful night!
Sweet be thy rest to the weary,
Making the dull heart and dreary
Laugh in a dream of delight—
Wonderful night!

Wonderful night!
Let me as long as life lingers
Sing with the cherubim singers,
Glory to God in the height;"
Wonderful night!

3

THE BOY AND THE FLOWERS.

WILLIE, with a spirit light, was a happy
　　little child,
Playing near a fountain bright, playing with
　　the flowers wild;
Where they grew he lightly stepped, cautious
　　not a leaf to crush,
Then about the fountain leaped, shouting at
　　its merry gush.

While the shining waters welled, laughing as
　　they bubbled up,
In his little hand he held, closely clasped, his
　　silver cup;
Now he dipped it in to fill, now he bore it to
　　the flowers,
Through his fingers let it spill, all it held, in
　　mimic showers.

"Open, pretty buds," said he—"open to the
　　air and sun;
So to-morrow I may see what my little rain
　　has done;

Yes you will, you will I know, for the drink
    I give you now,
Burst your little cups and blow while I'm
    gone and can't tell how.

" I just wish that I could see how God's finger
    touches you,
When your sides unclasp, and free let the
    spice and petals through ;
I would watch you all the night, nor in dark-
    ness be afraid,
Only once to see aright how a pretty flower
    is made.

" Now remember, I shall come in the morn-
    ing from my bed,
Here to find among you some with their
    brightest colors spread."
To his buds he hastened out, at the dewy
    morning hour,
Crying with a joyful shout, " God has made
    each bud a flower."

Precious must the ready faith of the little
    children be
In the sight of Him who saith, "Suffer them
    to come to me."
Answered by the smile of heaven is the in-
    fant's offering found,
Though a cup of water given only to the
    thirsty ground.

MY MOTHER.

Who fed me from her gentle breast,
And hushed me in her arms to rest,
And on my cheek sweet kisses prest?
                  My mother!

When sleep forsook my open eye,
Who was it sung sweet hushaby,
And rocked me that I should not cry?
                  My mother!

Who sat and watched my infant head
When sleeping on my cradle bed,
And tears of sweet affection shed?
                  My mother!

When pain and sickness made me cry,
Who gazed upon my heavy eye,
And wept for fear that I should die?
                    My mother!

Who dressed my doll in clothes so gay,
And taught me pretty how to play,
And minded all I had to say?
                    My mother!

Who ran to help me when I fell,
And would some pretty story tell,
Or kiss the place to make it well?
                    My mother!

Who taught my infant lips to pray,
And love God's holy book and day,
And walk in wisdom's pleasant way?
                    My mother!

And can I ever cease to be
Affectionate and kind to thee,
Who was so very kind to me,
                    My mother?

3 *

Ah no! the thought I cannot bear;
And if God please my life to spare,
I hope I shall reward thy care,
                    My mother!

When thou art feeble, old and gray
My healthy arm shall be thy stay,
And I will soothe thy pains away,
                    My mother!

And when I see thee hang thy head,
'Twill be my turn to watch thy bed,
And tears of sweet affection shed,
                    My mother!

For God, who lives above the skies,
Would look with vengeance in his eyes
If I should ever dare despise
                    My mother!

THE COMMANDMENTS.

THIS is the just and great command :
  To love thy God above ;
And this the second : As thyself
  Thy neighbor thou shalt love.

Who is thy neighbor?   He who wants
  The help which thou canst give ;
And both the law and prophets say,
  "This do, and thou shalt live."

ROSCOE.

THE CHILDREN'S HYMN.

SING to the Lord the children's hymn ;
  His gentle love declare,
Who bends amid the cherubim
  To hear the children's prayer.

He at a mother's breast was fed,
  Though God's own Son was he ;
He learned the first small words he said,
  Meek, at his mother's knee.

He held us to his mighty breast,
  The children of the earth ;
He lifted up his hands and blessed
  The babes of human birth.

Although he is the Son of God,
  Our gracious Saviour too,
The scenes we tread his footsteps trod,
  The paths of youth he knew.

And from the stars his face will turn
  On us with glances mild ;
The angels of his presence yearn
  To bless the little child.

THE SWEET STORY.

I THINK, when I read that sweet story of
    old,
When Jesus was here among men—
How he called little children like lambs to
    his fold—
I should like to have been with him then.

I wish that his hands had been placed on my
    head,
And his arms had been thrown around me;
And that I might have seen his kind look
    when he said,
"Let the little ones come unto me."

But still to his footstool in prayer I may go,
    And ask for a share of his love;
And if I thus earnestly seek him below,
    I shall see him and hear him above—

In that beautiful place he has gone to pre-
    pare
For all who are washed and forgiven;
And many dear children are gathering there,
    For of such is the kingdom of heaven.

THE LOVE OF CHRIST.

Jesus loves me—this I know,
For the Bible tells me so;
Little ones to him belong—
They are weak, but he is strong.

Jesus loves me—he who died
Heaven's gate to open wide;
He will wash away my sin:
Let his little child come in.

Jesus loves me—loves me still,
Though I'm very weak and ill;
From his shining throne on high
Comes to watch me where I lie.

Jesus loves me—he will stay
Close beside me all the way;
If I love him when I die,
He will take me home on high.

—◆—

LITTLE THINGS.

LITTLE drops of water, little grains of sand,
Make the mighty ocean and the pleasant
land;

And the little moments, humble though they
be,
Make the mighty ages of Eternity.

So our little errors lead the soul astray
From the paths of virtue, oft in sin to stray.

Little deeds of kindness, little words of love,
Make our earth an Eden like the heaven
    above.

CRADLE HYMN.

Hush, my dear! lie still and slumber;
    Holy angels guard thy bed,
Heavenly blessings without number
    Gently falling on thy head.

Sleep, my babe! thy food and raiment,
    House and home thy friends provide;
And without thy care or payment
    All thy wants are well supplied.

Soft and easy is thy cradle;
    Coarse and hard thy Saviour lay,
When his birth-place was a stable,
    And his softest bed was hay.

Mayst thou live to know and fear him,
　Trust and love him all thy days;
Then go dwell for ever near him,
　See his face and sing his praise.

I could give thee thousand kisses,
　Hoping what I most desire;
Not a mother's fondest wishes
　Can to greater joys aspire.

Dr. Watts.

OUR FATHER.

DEAREST Father! dwelling high,
Far above the starry sky;
Seated on thy shining throne,
Hear me pray, "Thy kingdom come."

Hear me bless his holy name
Who a little child became—
Bless the Spirit thou hast given,
God most high, in earth and heaven.

Wicked I have often been;
Oh, forgive me every sin,
Even as I forgive each one
Who to me a wrong has done.

Keep me from each evil thought,
For the Lord my soul has bought;
Me from powers of evil keep
When I wake and when I sleep.

I, thy little child, would bring
Prayers and praises to my King;
Let my heart cease singing never,
"Glory be to God for ever."

HELEN LOUISA BROWN.

THE TWO PENNIES.

A PENNY I have, it is all my own,
Little Charlotte exclaimed in a lively tone;
I cannot do much with a penny, I fear,
But I'll buy myself something to eat or to
    wear.

4

A penny I have, little Mary said,
And she thoughtfully raised her hand to her
    head;
Both missions and schools need money, I
    know,
But I fear it is little my penny can do.

So Charlotte ran off and some apples she
    bought,
While Mary her mite to the mission-box
    brought;
And which of them, think you, more cheer-
    fully smiled?
And which of the two was the happier child?

                            M. A. STODDARD.

—◆—

TWINKLE, LITTLE STAR.

TWINKLE, twinkle, little star;
How I wonder what you are,
Up above the world so high,
Like a diamond in the sky!
When the shining sun is set,
When the grass with dew is wet,

Then you show your little light,
Twinkle, twinkle, all the night.
In the dark blue sky you keep,
And often through my curtains peep,
For you never shut your eye
Till the sun is in the sky.

———◦◦◦———

BUSY BEE.

How doth the little busy bee
    Improve each shining hour,
And gather honey all the day,
    From every opening flower!
How skillfully she builds her cell,
    How neat she lays her wax,
And labors hard to start it well,
    With the sweet food she makes!
In works of labor or of skill
    I would be busy too;
For Satan finds some mischief still
    For idle hands to do.

ISAAC WATTS.

VESPER.

Thou that rulest earth and heaven,
　　Darkness and light,
Who the day for toil hast given,
　　For rest the night!
May thine angel-guards defend us,
Slumbers sweet thy mercy send us,
Holy hopes and dreams attend us,
　　This livelong night.

Reginald Heber.

EVENING HYMN.

Glory to thee, my God, this night,
For all the blessings of the light;
Keep me, oh keep me, King of kings,
Beneath the shadow of thy wings.

Forgive me, Lord, through thy dear Son,
The ills which I this day have done;
That with the world, myself and thee,
I, ere I sleep, at peace may be.

Teach me to live that I may dread
The grave as little as my bed;
Teach me to die, that so I may
Rise joyful at the judgment-day.

Be thou my Guardian while I sleep;
Thy watchful station near me keep;
My heart with love celestial fill,
And guard me from the approach of ill.

Lord, let my heart for ever share
The bliss of thy paternal care;
'Tis heaven on earth, 'tis heaven above,
To see thy face, to sing thy love.

BISHOP KEN.

THE BABY.

ANOTHER little wave upon the sea of life,
Another soul to save amid its toil and strife;
Two more little feet to walk the dusty road,
To choose where two paths meet—the narrow
    and the broad.

4 *

Two more little hands to work for good or
    ill;
Two more little eyes, another little will;
Another heart to love, receiving love again;
And so the baby came, a thing of joy and
    pain.

Mrs. Lucy E. Akerman.

CRADLE HYMN.

Sweet baby, sleep! what ails my dear?
    What ails my darling thus to cry?
Be still, my child, and lend thine ear
    To hear me sing thy lullaby:
My pretty lamb, forbear to weep,
Be still, my dear; sweet baby, sleep.

Thou blessed soul, what canst thou fear?
    What thing to thee can mischief do?
Thy God is now thy Father dear,
    His holy Church thy mother too;
Sweet baby, then forbear to weep,
Be still, my babe; sweet baby, sleep.

Whilst thus thy lullaby I sing,
   For thee great blessings ripening be;
Thine eldest Brother is a King,
   And hath a kingdom bought for thee;
Sweet baby, then forbear to weep,
Be still, my babe; sweet baby, sleep.

Sweet baby, sleep, and nothing fear,
   For whosoever thee offends
By thy Protector threatened are,
   And God and angels are thy friends;
Sweet baby, then forbear to weep,
Be still, my babe; sweet baby, sleep.

GEORGE WITHERS.

TO-DAY AND TO-MORROW.

TO-DAY! a lisping child, with hair all golden,
   And blue of summer morning in his eyes,
And cheeks aglow with kisses of new loving,
   Sees old things new, with ignorant surprise;
   To-morrow! and he knows the songs they
     sing in Paradise.

To-day! a youth in pride of early manhood,
  With light of far-off hope upon his brow,
With eager expectation of the coming,
  And wild impatience of the loitering now;
  To-morrow! he hath touched the throne
    at which all angels bow.

To-day! an old man lingers in his sadness;
  Great griefs have digged deep furrows in
    his cheeks;
A cold grave, with the long-ago departed,
  In stammering words, is all the boon he
    seeks;
  To-morrow! with unfaltering lips the joy
    of heaven he speaks.

WORK AND PLAY.

WORK while you work, play while you play;
That is the way to be cheerful and gay;
All that you do, do with your might—
Things done by halves are never done right.

BESSIE BELL.

DEAR mother, why do all the girls
  Love little Bessie Bell?
I've often thought it o'er and o'er,
  And yet I cannot tell.
My favorite cousin always was
  Dear gentle cousin Bess;
But why the others love her so
  Indeed I cannot guess.

They hear her gentle voice, my child,
  And see her mild, soft eye
Beaming around on every one
  With love and sympathy;
They see her striving every hour
  For others' happiness:
These are some reasons why the girls
  So love dear little Bess.

Her widowed mother's heart she cheers
  With love and tenderness,
And by her daily walk with God
  And growth in holiness;

Sweet Bessie is a Christian child,
    She loves the Saviour dear:
One of the lambs of his own flock,
    She has no want or fear.

Money, which other children spend
    In candy, toys or cakes,
She carries to the poor and sick—
    She loves them for Christ's sake.
Poor old blind Dinah down the lane
    She reads to every day,
And ne'er forgets it, though dear Bess
    Is very fond of play.

And now, my little daughter dear,
    Would you be loved like Bess?
Go ask of God to change your heart
    From pride to humbleness.
Better than beauty, rank or gold
    To be like little Bess,
Clothed in the spotless garment
    Of the Saviour's righteousness.

OUR BABY.

To-day we cut the fragrant sod with trem-
    bling hands asunder,
And lay this well-beloved of God, our dear
    dead baby, under;
O hearts that ache, and ache afresh! O
    tears too blindly raining!
Our hearts are weak, yet, being flesh, too
    strong for our restraining.

Sleep, darling, sleep! cold rains shall steep
    thy little turf-made dwelling;
Thou wilt not know—so far below—what
    winds and storms are swelling;
And birds shall sing in the warm spring, and
    flowers bloom about thee;
Thou wilt not heed them, love! but oh the
    loneliness without thee!

Father, we will be comforted; thou wast the
    gracious Giver;
We yield her up—not dead, not dead—to
    dwell with thee for ever;

Take thou our child, ours for a day; thine
    while the ages blossom;
This little shining head we lay in the Re-
    deemer's bosom.

TWO LITTLE ROBINS.

Two Robin Redbreasts built their nest
    Within a hollow tree;
The hen sat quietly at home,
    The cock sang merrily;
And all the little young ones said,
    "We, wee—we, wee—we, wee."

One day the sun was warm and bright,
    And shining in the sky;
Cock Robin said, "My little dears,
    'Tis time you learned to fly,"
And all the little young ones said,
    "We'll try—we'll try—we'll try."

I know a child, and who she is
    I'll tell you by and by;
When mamma says, "Do this or that,"
    She says, "What for?" and "Why?"
She'd be a better child by far
    If she would say, "I'll try."

THE GRAIN OF CORN AND THE PENNY.

A GRAIN of corn an infant's hand
May plant upon an inch of land,
Whence twenty stalks may spring, and yield
Enough to stock a little field;
The harvest of that field might then
Be multiplied to ten times ten,
Which, sown thrice more, would furnish bread
Wherewith an army might be fed.

A penny is a little thing,
Which even the poor man's child may fling
Into the treasury of heaven,
And make it worth as much as seven;
As seven?—nay, worth its weight in gold;
And that increased a million-fold.

5

For lo! a penny tract applied
But well, may save a soul alive;
That soul can scarce be saved alone:
It must, it will, its bliss make known.
" Come," it will cry, "and you shall see
What great things God hath done for me."
Hundreds that joyful sound may hear—
Hear with the heart as well as ear—
And these to thousands more proclaim
Salvation in the " only name;"
Till every tongue and tribe shall call
On Jesus as the Lord of all.

J. MONTGOMERY.

LITTLE DEEDS.

NOT mighty deeds make up the sum of
    happiness below,
But little acts of kindliness that any child
    may show;
A merry sound to cheer the babe and drive
    away his fear,
A word of childish sympathy, to dry the
    childish tear.

A glass of water timely brought, an offered
    easy-chair ;
A turning of the window blind, that all may
    feel the air ;
A shading of the lamp for eyes too weak the
    light to bear ;
An early flower bestowed unasked, a light
    and cautious tread ;
A voice to gentle whispers hushed to spare
    an aching head ;
The little ones amused for hours, or patient
    slowly led.

Oh deeds like these, though little things, un-
    selfish love disclose,
As fragrant perfume on the air reveals the
    hidden rose ;
Our heavenly Father loves to see these pre-
    cious fruits of love ;
And those who are unselfish here shall dwell
    with him above.

GOOD-NIGHT AND GOOD-MORNING.

A DEAR little girl sat under a tree,
Sewing as long as her eyes could see;
Then smoothed her work and folded it right,
And said, "Dear work, good-night! good-
     night!"

Such a number of rooks came over her head,
Crying, Caw, caw, caw, on their way to bed;
She said, as she watched their curious flight,
"Little black things, good-night! good-
     night!"

The horses neighed, the oxen lowed,
The sheep's bleat, bleat, came over the road,
All seeming to say with quiet delight,
"Good little girl! good-night! good-night!"

She did not say to the sun, Good-night!
Though she saw him there like a ball of
     light;
For she knew he had God's time to keep
All over the world, and never could sleep.

The tall pink foxglove bowed his head,
The violets curtsied and went to bed;
And good little Lucy tied up her hair,
And said on her knees her favorite prayer.

And while on her pillow she softly lay,
She knew nothing more till again it was day,
And all things said to the beautiful sun,
" Good-morning! good-morning! our work is
    begun."
                                    R. M. MILNES.

THE BLESSING OF LABOR.

LABOR gives rest from the sorrows that
    greet us—
Rest from the petty vexations that meet us;
Rest from sin-promptings that ever entreat
    us;
Rest from temptations that lure us to ill;
Work! and pure slumbers shall wait on thy
    pillow;
Work! thou shalt ride over care's coming
    billow,
Work with a stout heart and resolute will.
5 *

Work for some good, be it ever so slowly,
Cherish some plant, be it ever so lowly;
Labor! Such labor is noble and holy;
    Let thy good deeds be thy prayer to thy
      God.
Mrs. Osgood.

SPEAK GENTLY.

Speak gently: it is better far
    To rule by love than fear;
Speak gently: let not harsh words mar
    The good we might do here.

Speak gently to the aged one:
    Grieve not the care-worn heart;
The sands of life are nearly run—
    Let such in peace depart.

Speak gently, kindly to the poor:
    Let no harsh tones be heard;
They have enough they must endure
    Without an unkind word.

Speak gently: 'tis a little thing
  Dropped in the heart's deep well;
The good, the joy that it may bring
  Eternity shall tell.

THE CHILD'S FIRST GRIEF.

Oh call my brother back to me;
  I cannot play alone;
The summer comes with flower and bee:
  Where has my brother gone?
The butterfly is glancing bright
  Across the sunbeam's track;
I care not now to chase his flight;
  Oh call my brother back.

"He would not hear thy voice, my child;
  He may not come to thee:
The face that once like spring-time smiled,
  On earth no more thou'lt see;
A rose's bright, brief life of joy,
  Such unto him was given;
Go, thou must play alone, my boy;
  Thy brother is in heaven."

And has he left his birds and flowers?
  And must I call in vain?
And through the long, long summer hours
  Will he not come again?
And by the brook and in the glade
  Are all our wanderings o'er?
Oh when my brother with me played
  Would I had loved him more!

MRS. HEMANS.

PRIDE AND HUMILITY.

How proud we are, how fond of show!
We call our clothing "rich" and "new,"
When the poor sheep and silkworm wore
The stuff that makes them long before.

The tulip and the butterfly
Wear a far gayer coat than I;
Let me be dressed fine as I will,
Flies, worms, birds, flowers surpass me still.

There is a pure and lovely dress
  I pray my God to give to me—
My Saviour's robe of righteousness,
  And for my crown, Humility.

EVENING HYMN.

JESUS, tender Shepherd, hear me;
  Bless thy little lambs to-night;
Through the darkness be thou near me,
  Watch my sleep till morning light.

All the day thy hand hast led me,
  And I thank thee for thy care;
Thou hast clothed me, warmed me, fed me;
  Listen to my evening prayer.

Let my sins be all forgiven,
  Bless the friends I love so well;
Take me when I die to heaven,
  Happy there with thee to dwell.

M. L. DUNCAN.

TOUCH NOT, TASTE NOT.

TOUCH not the tempting cup, my boy, though
    urged by friend or foe;
Dare when the tempter urges most, dare
    nobly say No! no!
  The warning given from on high
  Shall tell your soul the reason why.

Touch not the tempting cup, my boy, in
    righteousness be brave,
Take not the first, the fatal step toward a
    drunkard's grave;
  The widow's groan, the orphan's sigh
  Shall tell your soul the reason why.

ROBINS.

A VERY pretty sight this morning I did see,
Four little robins sitting on a tree;
A bright red cherry one of them did pull;
It was large and ripe and very beautiful.

So he gave it to his mate as if wishing her
    to see,
And passed it along to each of the three;
And then they all began to eat a little piece,
Stopping to whistle, Oh how very nice!

And when they had eaten it all so lovingly,
They flew away again, singing right merrily;
These little robins, living so happily,
Teach many lessons sweet and dear to me.

How boys can harm them I do not know,
And be so cruel to them and make them fear
us so.

MISS TAYLOR.

———◦◦◦———

MRS. LOFTY AND I

MRS. LOFTY keeps a carriage—so do I;
She has dapple grays to draw it—none have I;
She's no prouder with her coachman than
am I
With my blue-eyed, laughing baby, trund-
ling by;
I hide his face lest she should see
The cherub boy, and envy me.

Mrs. Lofty has her jewels—so have I;
She wears hers upon her bosom—inside I;
She will leave hers at death's portals by
and by;
I shall bear the treasure with me when I
die;
For I have love and she has gold;
She counts her wealth, mine can't be told.

Her fine husband has white fingers—mine
 has not;
He could give his bride a palace—mine a cot;
Hers comes home beneath the starlight—ne'er
 cares she;
Mine comes in the purple twilight, kisses me,
 And prays that He who turns life's sands
 Will hold his loved ones in his hands.

She has those that love her station—none
 have I;
But I've one true heart beside me—glad am I;
I'd not change it for a kingdom, no not I;
God will weigh it in his balance, by and by;
 And then the difference will define
 'Twixt Mrs. Lofty's wealth and mine.

LET IT PASS.

BE not swift to take offence—let it pass!
Anger is a foe to sense—let it pass!
Brood not darkly o'er a wrong,
Which will disappear ere long;
Rather sing this cheery song: Let it pass!
 let it pass!

Strife corrodes the purest mind; let it pass!
As the unregarded wind, let it pass!
Any vulgar souls that live
May condemn without reprieve;
'Tis the noble who forgive; let it pass! let
     it pass!

Echo not an angry word; let it pass!
Think how often you have erred; let it pass!
Since our joys must pass away
Like the dew-drops on the spray,
Wherefore should our sorrows stay? let them
     pass! let them pass!

If for good you've taken ill; let it pass!
Oh be kind and gentle still; let it pass!
Time at last makes all things straight;
Let us not resent, but wait,
And our triumph shall be great; let it pass!
     let it pass!

Bid your anger to depart; let it pass!
Lay these homely words to heart; let it pass!

6

Follow not the giddy throng;
Better to be wronged than wrong;
Therefore sing the cheery song, let it pass!
    let it pass!

ALL THE YEAR ROUND.

SHADOWS.

THE candles are lighted, the fire blazes
    bright;
  The curtains are drawn to keep out the
    cold air;
What makes you so grave, little darling, to-
    night?
  And where is your smile, little quiet one?
    where?

Mamma, I see something so dark on the
    wall;
  It moves up and down and it looks very
    strange;
Sometimes it is large and sometimes it is
    small;
  Pray tell me what is it, and why does it
    change?

It's only my shadow that puzzles you so,
  And there is your own close beside it, my
     love;
Now run round the room, it will go where
     you go;
  When you sit, 'twill be still; when you
     rise, it will move.

These wonderful shadows are made by the
     light
  From the fire and from candles, upon us
     that falls;
Were we not sitting here, all that place would
     be bright,
  But the light can't shine through us, you
     know, on the walls.

And when you are out some fine day in the
     sun,
  I'll take you where shadows of apple trees
     lie;
And houses and cottages too, every one
  Casts a shade when the sun shineth bright
     in the sky.

Now hold up your mouth, and give me a
    sweet kiss;
  Our shadows kiss too, don't you see it
    quite plain?
"Oh yes—thank you, mamma, for telling me
    this;
  I shall not be afraid of a shadow again."

M. L. DUNCAN.

"PATCHIE."

THE bell had rung, the school was out,
  And from the hall with busy feet
The boys rushed forth with laugh and shout,
  And crowded through the village street,
Like prisoners from their cells broke loose, .
Escaping from the calaboose.

Across the street, and all alone,
  A small boy walked with rapid gait,
Like one unknowing and unknown,
  With head erect and form so straight;
He heeded not the crowd that cried,
"See ' Patchie' on the other side!"

I wondered much why this should be,
  But when I looked I knew too well:
The noblest of them all was he;
  But sad to think, more sad to tell,
He from the crowd had been detached
Because his pantaloons were patched!

No answering word escaped him there;
  I watched him as he climbed the hill,
Then thought, "Each other's burdens bear,
  And thus the law of Christ fulfill;"
And so I joined him on the road,
Hoping to lighten his sad load.

I spoke in loving words and kind;
  He, smiling, looked up in my face—
He had a true and noble mind—
  And answered with a manly grace,
"My father, sir, has long been dead,
And mother earns our daily bread.

"To school she sends me every day,
  I do the best there that I can,
And mother says she'll get her pay
  When I grow up to be a man;
  6 *

And, sir, I hope that I shall be
. All that my mother wishes me.

"They call me 'Patchie;' I don't care,"
    Said he, while passing through the gate;
" It's what we are, not what we wear,
    That makes us good and makes us great;"
He touched his cap, and said good-night:
I whispered, " Noble, brave and right."

I started on my homeward way:
    Not only boys, but men, I thought,
Pass by the poor ones every day;
    Only the rich and grand are sought;
This world, so full of foolish pride,
Puts "Patchie" on the other side.

                                    MRS. S. T. PERRY.

KATIE'S DREAM.

IT was a warm and sultry afternoon,
    And little Katie's weary, tangled head
Fell slowly down upon her open book,
    And Katie slept as sound as if in bed.

And in her dreams her little brother came
  (Dear little Willie, who to heaven had
      gone),
And pressed his face to hers, and called her
      name
With many a loving and endearing tone.

And she had kissed his little rosy cheek,
  Whose pretty dimples still were lingering
      there,
Looked in his laughing, deep blue eyes once
      more,
  Played with the ringlets of his golden hair.

"Stay with me, Willie! darling boy!" she
      cried;
  " For though the angels are so bright and
      fair,
They cannot love you as your sister loves—
  Oh, Willie dear, do not stay always there!"

Just then a sudden stir was in the room,
  And on her ear the teacher's loud voice
      broke,

"Children, a storm is coming! hasten home;"
   Willie went back to heaven, and Katie
     woke!

She rubbed her eyes, and there came rolling
     down
   Great tears upon her flushed and fevered
     cheek.
" Why, what's the matter dear?" said little
     Bell,
   But Katie only sobbed, and could not
     speak.

At length she said, "Oh, Bell, my Willie
     came—
   But now I know it only was a dream;
For mother says he'll never come to us,
   But some day we shall go away to him."

" Why didn't you go and see him, then?"
     said Bell.
   " Why, dear, I do not know the way;
You know I was so very sick myself,
   I could not see where they all went that
     day."

"Then I can tell you, darling, where he's
    gone;
I watched them till they turned into the
    gate."
"What, heaven's gate?" said Katy. "Oh
    let's run,
And find dear Willie ere it be too late!"

Then hand in hand the eager children ran
    To find the gate of heaven and little Will;
The rain in torrents beat upon their heads,
    But only made them run the faster still.

"There! that's the place!" said Bell, as up-
    ward rose
    The cemetery's heavy iron gate.
"Now, hurry, Katie! hurry! for you know
    Our mother said we must not stay out late."

The rain beat on the little curly head
    As loud she knocked, then louder than
    before:
"Willie! dear Willie! sister Katie calls,
    Please bring the key and open heaven's
    door!"

"I hear him, Bell! I hear his little feet!"
  And smiles broke o'er her face like sun
    through cloud.
"No, darling, 'tis the pattering rain-drops'
    beat."
  "Well, now, I'll call him very loud."

"Willie!" the little piercing voice then cried,
  With half a panting sob and half a shriek—
"Willie, do come! poor sister's wet and tired,
  Waiting so long to kiss your little cheek."

"Perhaps he's playing with the angels, dear!"
  · said Bell,
    "And does not hear when you his name
      repeat."
"Ah, now he's coming, sure! for I know well
  The pretty patter of his baby feet.

"No, no, he does not come. Oh, little Will,
  How long you leave me standing in the
    rain!
Bell, you run home, but I must wait here
    still,
  For I can never find the way again."

At length came those who long had searched,
    and late
  For Katie through the darkness and the
    storm;
Down on the ground, close by the graveyard
    gate,
  They found the little senseless, prostrate
    form.

He did not come to her, but she had gone
  To him, where there is no more cloud nor
    sea,
And through earth's darkness, gloom and
    pelting storm
  Kate had found heaven's gate, and entered
    in.

From thee, sweet Katie, let us learn aright—
Not at death's door to seek the way to
    light,
For not to sight, but unto faith, 'tis given,
To find the golden gate that leads to hea-
    ven.

                        S. H. B.

CHRIST AND THE LITTLE ONES.

"The Master has come over Jordan,"
    Said Hannah, the mother, one day;
"He is healing the people who throng him
    With a touch of his finger, they say."

"And now I shall carry the children,
    Little Rachel, and Samuel, and John;
I shall carry the baby Esther,
    For the Lord to look upon."

The father looked at her kindly,
    But he shook his head and smiled:
"Now who but a doting mother
    Would think of a thing so wild?"

"If the children were tortured by demons
    Or dying of fever, 'twere well,
Or had they the taint of the leper,
    Like many in Israel."

"Nay, do not hinder me, Nathan;
    I feel such a burden of care
If I carry it to the Master,
    Perhaps I shall leave it there.

" If he lay his hand on the children,
  My heart will be lighter I know,
For a blessing for ever and ever
  Will follow them as they go."

So over the hills of Judah,
  Along by the vine-rows green,
With Rachel asleep on her bosom,
  And Esther her brothers between,

'Mong the people who hung on his teaching,
  Or waited his touch and his word,
Through the row of proud Pharisees listening,
  She pressed to the feet of the Lord.

" Now why should'st thou hinder the Master,"
  Said Peter, " with children like these?
Seest not how from morning till evening
  He toucheth and healeth disease?"

Then Christ said, " Forbid not the children;
  Permit them to come unto me;"
And he took in his arms little Esther,
  And Rachel he set on his knee.

And the heavy heart of the mother
    Was lifted all earth-care above,
As he laid his hands on the brothers
    And blessed them with tenderest love—

As he said of the babe in his bosom,
    "Of such is the kingdom of heaven;"
And strength for all duty and trial
    That hour to her spirit was given.

———❦———

THE WOOD-MOUSE.

Do you know the little wood-mouse,
    The pretty little thing
That sits among the forest leaves
    Beside the forest spring?

Its fur is as red as the chestnut,
    And it is small and slim;
It leads a life most innocent
    Within the forest dim.

'Tis a timid, gentle creature,
  And seldom comes in sight;
It has a long and wiry tail,
  And eyes both black and bright.

It makes its nest of soft, dry moss
  In a hole so deep and strong;
And there it sleeps secure and warm
  The dreary winter long.

And though it keeps no almanac,
  It knows when flowers are springing;
And waketh to its summer life
  When nightingales are singing.

Upon the boughs the squirrel sits,
  The wood-mouse plays below;
And plenty of food it finds itself
  Where the beech and chestnut grow.

In the hedge-sparrow's nest he sits
  When its summer brood is fled,
And picks the berries from the bough
  Of the hawthorn overhead.

I saw a little wood-mouse once,
　Like a monarch in his hall,
With the green, green moss beneath his feet,
　Sit under a mushroom tall.

I saw him sit and his dinner eat
　All under the forest-tree—
His dinner of chestnuts ripe and red;
　And he ate it heartily.

I wish you could have seen him there;
　It did my spirit good
To see the small thing God had made
　Thus eating in the wood.

I saw that he regardeth them—
　Those creatures weak and small;
Their table in the wild is spread
　By Him who cares for all.

MARY HOWITT.

The English Child.

AN ENGLISH CHILD IN THE DAYS OF WICKLIFFE.

A LITTLE child, she read a book beside an
    open door,
And as she read page after page she won-
    dered more and more;
Her little finger carefully went pointing out
    the place;
Her golden locks hung drooping down and
    shadowed half her face.

The open book lay on her knee; her eyes on
    it were bent,
And as she read page after page, her color
    came and went;
She sat upon a mossy stone, an open door
    beside,
And round, for miles on every side, stretched
    out a forest wide.

The summer sun shone on the trees, the deer
    lay in the shade,
And overhead the singing birds their pleas-
    ant clamor made;

7 *

There was no garden round about, yet flowers
    were growing free,
The cowslip and the daffodil, upon the forest
    lea.

The butterfly went flitting by, the bees were
    in the flowers,
But the little child sat steadfastly as she had
    sat for hours.
" Why sit ye here, my little maid ?" an aged
    pilgrim spake ;
The child looked upward from her book, like
    one but just awake.

Back fell her locks of golden hair, and
    solemn was her look,
And thus she answered witlessly : "Oh, sir,
    I read this book."
" And what is there within that book to win
    a child like thee ?
Up ! join thy mates, the singing-birds, and
    frolic like the bee."

"Nay, sir! I cannot leave the book : I love it
    more than play ;
I have read legends, but this one saw never
    till to-day ;
And there is something in this book that
    makes all care begone,
And yet I weep, I know not why, as I go
    reading on."

"Who art thou, child, that thou shouldst
    read a book with so much heed?
Books are for clerks; the king himself has
    much ado to read."
"My father is a forester, a bowman keen
    and good ;
He keeps the deer within their bounds, and
    worketh in the wood.

"My mother died at Candlemas; the flowers
    are all in blow,
Upon her grave at Allenby, down in the vale
    below."

This said, unto her book she turned as steadfast as before.
"Nay!" said the pilgrim, "nay not yet, and
you must tell me more.

"Who was it taught you thus to read?"
"Ah, sir, it was my mother;
She taught me both to read and spell, and so
she taught my brother;
My brother dwelt at Allenby, with the good
monk alway,
And this new book he brought to me, but
only for one day.

"Oh, sir, it is a wondrous book—better than
Charlemagne;
And be you pleased to leave me now, I'll
read in it again."
"Nay, read to me," the pilgrim said; and
the little child went on
To read of Christ, as is set forth in the
gospel of St. John.

On, on she read, and gentle tears adown her
    cheeks did glide;
The pilgrim sat with bended head, and he
    wept by her side;
" I've heard," said he, " the archbishop—I've
    heard the Pope at Rome—
But never did their spoken words thus to
    my spirit come.

" The book, it is a blessed book; its name,
    what may it be?"
Said she, "They are the words of Christ that
    I have read to thee,
Now done into the English tongue for folks
    unlearned as me."

" Give me the Book and let me read—my
    soul is strangely stirred;
They are such words of love and truth as
    I ne'er before have heard."
The little girl gave up the book, and the pil-
    grim old and brown
With reverend lips did kiss the page, then
    on the stone sat down.

And aye he read page after page; page after
  page he turned;
And as he read their blessed words his heart
  within him burned,
Still, still the book the old man read, as he
  would ne'er have done;
From the hour of noon he read the book
  until the set of sun.

The little child she brought him out a cake
  of wheaten bread,
And it lay unbroken at eventide, nor did he
  raise his head;
Then came the sturdy forester along the
  homeward track,
Whistling aloud a hunting-tune, with a slain
  deer on his back.

Loud greeting gave the forester unto the pilgrim poor;
The old man rose with thoughtful brow and
  entered at the door;

They two they sat them down to meat, and
    the pilgrim 'gan to tell
How he had eaten at Olivet and drank at
    Jacob's well.

And then he told him he had knelt where'er
    our Lord had prayed;
How he had in the garden been and the tomb
    where he was laid;
And then he turned unto the book and read
    in English plain
How Christ had died on Calvary—how he
    had risen again.

As water to the parchèd soul, as to the
    hungry bread,
So fell upon the woodman's soul each word
    the pilgrim read;
Thus through the midnight did they read
    until the dawn of day
And then came in the woodman's son to take
    the book away.

All quick and troubled was his speech; his
    face was pale with dread;
For he said the king had made a law that
    the book should not be read,
For it was such a fearful heresy, the holy
    abbot said.

MARY HOWITT.

THE TEMPEST AT SEA.

WE were crowded in the cabin,
    Not a soul would dare to sleep,
It was midnight on the waters,
    And a storm was on the deep.

'Tis a fearful thing in winter
    To be shattered by the blast,
And to hear the rattling trumpet
    Thunder, " Cut away the mast!"

So we shuddered there in silence,
    For the stoutest held his breath;
While the hungry sea was roaring,
    And the breakers talked with death.

As thus we sat in darkness,
  Each one busy in his prayers,
" We are lost !" the captain shouted,
  As he staggered down the stairs.

But his little daughter whispered,
  As she took his icy hand,
" Isn't God upon the ocean,
  Just the same as on the land ?"

Then we kissed the little maiden,
  And we spoke in better cheer,
And we anchored safe in harbor
  When the morn was shining clear.

                          J. T. FIELDS.

———◦◦◦———

THE LOST CHILD.

ALONE, beneath the heavy shade,
  In forest thick and wild,
With timid eye and footstep strayed
  A poor bewildered child ;
Along the cold swamp's weedy edge
  He held his devious way,

8

Where coiled and hissing in the hedge
  The hideous serpent lay :
The hungry wolf with cry of death
  Leaped past him in the chase ;
The wild deer lingered in his path
  To scan the stranger's face.

And pale and full of agony
  That little face appeared ;
And terror filled his soft blue eye
  At every sound he heard ;
His yellow curls were bare and wet,
  His little coat was torn,
And stains of blood were on his feet,
  By reckless travel worn :
His little heart was sick with fear,
  His brain was wild and weak,
And hunger-pains, so hard to bear,
  Had blenched his rosy cheek.

And still by every mossy spot
  Where pleasant berries hide,
He sought, and when he found them not,
  Oh bitterly he cried ;

Four days that tangled forest through
  He sought his home in vain;
Fond hearts were breaking there, he knew,
  To see his face again.
"Mother! O mother!" was his cry,
  Until his voice grew weak;
And throat and tongue were parched and dry,
  And then he could not speak.

The silent shades are gathering now
  With dark and dewy wings,
Forming in dell and valley low
  Dim shades of fearful things;
His frame with curdling horror shook,
  His heart grew cold as clay;
He crept into a sheltered nook,
  Crouched down and tried to pray;
And then he thought that God was near
  To watch above his bed,
And every agonizing fear
  And phantom horror fled.

The pangs of hunger died away,
  And grief withdrew its sting;

And slumber o'er his spirit lay,
   Soft as an angel's wing;
And then he dreamed sweet dreams of home,
   With all its love and bliss—
The rural feast, the lighted room,
   The mother's tender kiss;
The little face grew calm and white,
   His slumber still and deep;
Sweet boy, thy sorrows end to-night—
   Thou shalt not wake to weep.

"Mother," he whispered languidly,
   And hugged the dewy sod;
'Tis done! he wakes in ecstasy,
   And sees the face of God;
Tell us, ye white-haired wanderers
   In life's dark devious ways,
Ye who have sown your path with tears
   So many weary days,
Ought we to mourn for him who lies
   In that wild dell alone—
Whose weary feet and weeping eyes,
   Have found their rest so soon?

MRS. PIERSON.

THE LITTLE MATCH-GIRL.

LITTLE GRETCHEN, little Gretchen
  Wanders up and down the street;
The snow is on her yellow hairs,
  The frost is at her feet;
The rows of long dark houses
  Without look cold and damp
Beneath the struggling moonbeams,
  By the flicker of the lamp!

The clouds ride fast as horses,
  The wind blows from the north,
But no one cares for Gretchen,
  And no one looketh forth
Within the lighted houses
  Are merry faces bright,
And happy hearts are watching out
  The Old Year's latest night.

The board is spread with plenty
  Where the smiling kindred meet;
But the frost lies on the pavement
  Beneath poor Gretchen's feet;

8 *

With the little box of matches
, No one had bought that day,
And the thin, thin, tattered mantle
The wind blows every way.

She clingeth to the railing,
    She shivers in the gloom:
There are parents sitting snugly
    By firelight in the room;
And groups of busy children—
    Withdrawing just the tips
Of rosy fingers, pressed in vain
    Against their bursting lips—

With grave and earnest faces
    Are whispering to each other
Of presents for the New Year, made
    For father or for mother!
But no one speaks to Gretchen,
    And no one hears her speak,
No breath of little whispers
    Comes warmly to her cheek.

No little ones are round her:
    Ah me! that there should be,

With so much happiness on earth,
  So much of misery!
Surely they who are blessed
  Should scatter blessings round;
As laden boughs in autumn fling
  Their ripe fruits to the ground.

The best love man can offer
  To the God of Love, be sure,
Is kindness to his little ones,
  And bounty to his poor!
Little Gretchen, little Gretchen,
  Goes shivering on her way;
There's no one looketh out at her,
  There's no one bids her stay.

Her home is cold and desolate—
  No smile, no food, no fire,
But children clamorous for bread,
  And an impatient sire;
So she sits down in the angle
  Where two great houses meet,
And curleth up beneath her,
  For warmth, her little feet.

She looks upon the cold wall,
   And on the cold, cold sky,
And wonders if the shining stars
   Are bright fires up on high!
She heard a clock strike slowly
   Up high in a church tower,
With such a sad and solemn tone
   Telling the midnight hour.

And she thought, as she sat lonely
   And listened to the chimes,
Of wondrous things that she had loved
   To hear in bygone times;
She heard again the stories
   Her mother used to tell,
And the cradle-songs she used to sing
   When summer's twilight fell—

Of good men and of angels
   And of the Holy Child
Who was cradled in a manger,
   All in the winter wild;
Who was poor, and cold, and hungry,
   And desolate, and lone;

And she thought the singing told her
He was ever with his own!

"Oh if the poor and hungry
And weary ones are his,
How good of him to look on me
In such a place as this!"
Colder it grows and colder,
But she does not feel it now,
For the pressure at her heart
And the weight upon her brow.

But she struck one little match
On the wall so cold and bare,
That she might look around her
And see if he was there ;
And now the match was kindled,
And by the light it threw
It seemed to little Gretchen
The wall was cleft in two ;

And she could see the room within—
A room all warm and bright,
With the fire all red and glowing,
And the tapers all alight.

And there were kindred gathered
  Round a table richly spread
With heaps of goodly viands—
  Red wine and pleasant bread

She could smell the fragrant savor,
  She could hear what they did say;
Then all was darkness once again—
  The match had burned away.
She struck another quickly,
  And now she seemed to see,
Within the same warm chamber,
  A glorious Christmas tree.

The branches were all laden
  With things that children prize—
Nice gifts for boy and maiden,
  She saw them with her eyes.
She almost seemed to touch them,
  And join the welcome shout:
Then darkness fell around her,
  For the little match was out.

Another, yet another, she
  Has tried; they will not light,

Till all her little store she took
  And struck with all her might.

And the whole miserable place
  Was lighted with the glare,
And lo! there hung a little child
  Before her in the air.
There were blood-drops on his forehead,
  And a spear-wound in his side,
And cruel nail-prints in his feet
  And in his hands spread wide.

He looked on her so gently,
  She felt that he had known
Pain, hunger, cold and sorrow,
  All equal to her own.
He pointed to the laden board
  And to the Christmas tree,
Then up to the cold sky, and said,
  "Will Gretchen come with me?"

The poor child felt her pulses fall,
  She felt her eyeballs swim,
And a ringing sound was in her ears,
  Like her dead mother's hymn.

She folded both her thin cold hands,
    And turned from that bright board,
And from the golden gifts, and said,
    " With thee—with thee, O Lord !"

The chilly winter morning
    Breaks up in the dull skies,
O'er the city wrapped in vapor,
    On the spot where Gretchen lies.
In her scanty, tattered garments,
    With her back against the wall,
She sitteth cold and rigid,
    She answers not their call.

They have lifted her up fearfully,
    And shuddered as they said,
" It was a bitter, bitter night—
    The child is frozen dead !"

The angels sang their greeting
    For one more, redeemed from sin !

Men said, " It was a bitter night ;
    Would no one let her in ?"

And they shuddered as they spoke of her,
  And sighed : they could not see
How much of happiness there was
  With so much misery.

HANS ANDERSON.

THE BLACKBERRY-GIRL.

WHY, Phœbe, are you come so soon?
  Where are your berries, child?
You surely have not sold them all—
  You had a basket piled.

No, mother; as I climbed the fence
  The nearest way to town,
My apron caught upon the stake,
  And so I tumbled down.

I scratched my arm and tore my hair,
  But still would not complain;
And had my blackberries been safe,
  Should not have cared a grain.

9

But when I saw them on the ground
  All scattered by my side,
I picked my empty basket up,
  And down I sat and cried.

Just then a pretty little miss
  Chanced to be walking by;
She stopped, and, looking pitiful,
  She begged me not to cry.

Poor little girl, you fell, said she,
  And must be sadly hurt;
Oh no, I cried, but see my fruit
  All mixed with sand and dirt.

Well, do not grieve for that, said she;
  Go home and get some more:
Ah no, for I have stripped the vines—
  These were the last they bore.

My father, miss, is very poor,
  And works in yonder stall;
He has so many little ones
  He cannot clothe us all.

I always longed to go to church,
    But I could never go,
For when I asked him for a gown,
    He always answered, No.

There's not a father in the world
    Who loves his children more;
I'd get you one with all my heart,
    But, Phœbe, I am poor.

So, when the blackberries were ripe,
    He said to me one day,
Phœbe, if you will take the time
    That's given you for play,

And gather blackberries enough,
    And carry them to town,
To buy your bonnet and your shoes,
    I'll try to get a gown.

Oh, miss, I fairly jumped for joy,
    My spirits were so light;
And so when I had leave to play,
    I picked with all my might.

I sold enough to get my shoes,
    About a week ago;
And these, if they had not been spilt,
    Would buy my bonnet too.

But now they're gone, they all are gone,
    And I can get no more;
And Sundays I must stay at home,
    Just as I did before.

And, mother, then I cried again
    As hard as I could cry,
And looking up I saw the tear
    Was falling from her eye.

She caught her bonnet from her head,
    Here! here! she cried, take this;
No, no indeed—I fear your ma
    Would be offended, miss.

Mamma! no, never; she delights
    All sorrow to beguile,
And 'tis the sweetest joy she feels
    To make the wretched smile.

She taught me, when I had enough,
　To share it with the poor,
And never let a needy child
　Go empty from the door.

So take it, for you need not fear
　Offending her, you see;
I have another too, at home,
　And one's enough for me.

So then I took it; here it is—
　For pray what could I do?
And, mother, I shall love that miss
　As long as I love you.

———◦◦———

THE FATHER OF THE FATHERLESS.

I KNEW a widow very poor,
　Who four small children had;
The oldest was but six years old,
　A gentle, modest lad.
9 *

And very hard this widow toiled
　To feed her children four ;
A noble heart the mother had,
　Though she was very poor.

To labor she would leave her home ;
　Her children must be fed ;
And glad was she when she could buy
　A shilling's worth of bread.

And this was all the children had
　On any day to eat ;
They drank their water, ate their bread,
　But never tasted meat.

One day the snow was falling fast,
　And piercing was the air ;
I thought that I would go and see
　How these poor children were.

Ere long I reached their cheerless home ;
　'Twas searched by every breeze ;
When, going in, the eldest child
　I saw upon his knees.

I paused to listen to the boy;
  He never raised his head,
But still went on and said, "Give us
  This day our daily bread!"

I waited till the child was done,
  Still listening as he prayed;
And when he rose, I asked him, "Why
  That prayer he then had said."

"Why, sir," said he, "this morning, when
  My mother went away,
She wept because she said she had
  No bread for us to-day.

"She said we children now must starve,
  Our father being dead;
And then I told her not to cry,
  For I would get some bread.

"'Our Father!' sir, the prayer begins;
  Which made me think that he,
As we have no kind father here,
  Would our kind Father be.

" And then you know, sir, that the prayer
  Asks God for bread each day;
So in the corner, sir, I went;
  That was what made me pray."

I quickly left that wretched room
  And went with fleeting feet,
And very soon was back again
  With food enough to eat.

" I thought God heard me!" said the boy;
  I answered with a nod;
I could not speak, but much I thought
  Of that boy's faith in God.

Dr. Hanks.

LITTLE WILLIE AND THE APPLE.

LITTLE WILLIE stood under an apple-tree
  old—
The fruit was all shining with crimson and
  gold;
Hanging temptingly low, how he longed for
  a bite,
Though he knew if he took one, it wouldn't
  be right!

Said he, "I don't see why my father should
    say,
'Don't touch the old apple-tree Willie, to-
    day;'
I shouldn't have thought—now they're hang-
    ing so low—
When I asked for just one, he would answer
    me, 'No!'

"He would never find out if I took but just
    one;
And they do look so good shining out in the
    sun;
There are hundreds and hundreds, and he
    wouldn't miss
So paltry a little red apple as this."

He stretched forth his hand but a low,
    mournful strain
Came wandering dreamily over his brain;
In his bosom a beautiful harp had long laid,
That the angel of conscience quite frequently
    played.

And he sung, "Little Willie, beware! Oh
beware!
Your father has gone, but your Maker is
there;
How sad you would feel, if you heard the
Lord say,
'This dear little boy stole an apple to-day!'"

Then Willie turned round, and as still as a
mouse
Crept slowly and carefully into the house;
In his own little chamber he knelt down to
pray
That the Lord would forgive him, and please
not to say,
"Little Willie almost stole an apple to-day."

M. A. D.

A LOST DAY.

CALL that day lost whose setting sun
Sees at thy hand no good thing done.

LITTLE BESSIE.

HUG me closer, closer, mother;
　Put your arms around me tight;
I am cold and tired, mother;
　And I feel so strange to-night.
Something hurts me here, dear mother,
　Like a stone upon my breast;
Oh I wonder, wonder, mother,
　Why it is I cannot rest.

All the day, while you were working,
　As I lay upon my bed,
I was trying to be patient,
　And to think of what you said;
How the kind and blessed Jesus
　Loves his lambs to watch and keep;
And I wished he'd come and take me
　In his arms, that I might sleep.

Just before the lamp was lighted,
　Just before the children came,
While the room was very quiet,
　I heard some one call my name.

All at once the windows opened;
   In a field were lambs and sheep—
Some from out a brook were drinking,
   Some were lying fast asleep.

But I could not see the Saviour,
   Though I strained my eyes to see;
And I wondered, if he saw me,
   If he'd speak to such as me;
·In a moment I was looking
   On a world so bright and fair,
Which was full of little children,
   And they seemed so happy there.

They were singing, oh how sweetly!
   Sweeter songs I never heard;
They were singing sweeter, mother,
   Than can sing our little bird;
And while I my breath was holding, ·
   One so bright upon me smiled
That I knew it must be Jesus,
   And he said, " Come here, my child!"

" Come up here, my little Bessie—
   Come up here and live with me;

Where the children never suffer
  But are happier than you see !'
Then I thought of all you told me
  Of that bright and happy land ;
I was going when you called me,
  When you came and kissed my hand.

" And at first I felt so sorry
  You had called me ; I would go—
Oh to sleep and never suffer !
  Mother, don't be crying so ;
Hug me closer, closer mother !
  Put your arms around me tight ;
Oh how much I love you, mother,
  But I feel so strange to-night !"

And the mother pressed her closer
  To her overburdened breast ;
On the heart so near to breaking,
  Lay the heart so near at rest.
In the solemn hour of midnight,
  In the darkness calm and deep,
Lying on her mother's bosom,
  Little Bessie fell asleep.

A. D. F. RANDOLPH.

10

THE STRANGE CHILD'S CHRISTMAS.

THERE went a stranger child,
  As Christmas eve closed in,
Through the streets of a town whose
      windows shone
  With the warmth and light within.

It stopped at every house
  The Christmas trees to see,
On that festive night, when they shone so
      bright,
  And the child sighed bitterly.

The little child wept and said,
  "This night hath every one
A Christmas tree, that they glad may be,
  And I alone have none!"

" Ah, when I lived at home,
  From brother's and sister's hand
I had my share, but there's none to care
  For me in the stranger's land!

" Will no one let me in ?
No presents I would crave,
But to see the light, and the tree all bright,
And the gifts the others have !"

At shutters, and doors, and gate
She knocks with timid hand ;
But none will mark where alone in the dark
That little child doth stand !

Each father brings home gifts,
Each mother kind and mild ;
There is joy for all, but none will call
And welcome that lonely child.

" Father and mother are dead,
O Jesus, kind and dear,
I have no one now, there is none but thou,
For I am a stranger here !"

The poor child rubs her hands,
All frozen and numbed with cold,
And draws round her head, with shrinking
dread,
Her garments worn and old !

But see! another child
  Comes gliding through the street;
His robes are white, in his hands a light;
  He speaks, and his voice is sweet.

"Once on this earth, a child,
  I lived as thou livest yet;
Though all turn away from thee this day,
  Yet I will not forget.

"Each child with equal love
  I hold beneath my care,
In the street's dull gloom, in the lighted
    room
  I am with them everywhere.

"Here in the darkness dim,
  I will show thee, child, thy tree;
Those that spread their light through
    chambers bright
  Are not so fair to see!"

Then with his white hand points
  The Christ-child to the sky;

And lo ! ajar, with each lamp a star,
  A tree gleamed there on high.

So far, and yet so near,
  The lights shone overhead ;
And all was well, for the child could tell
  For whom that tree was spread.

She gazed as in a dream,
  And angels bent and smiled ;
And with outstretched hand to that bright-
    er land
  They carried the stranger child.

And the little one went home,
  With her Saviour Christ to stay ;
All the hunger and cold and the pain of
    old
  Forgotten and passed away.

FROM THE GERMAN.

10 *

THE BLIND BOY.

It was a blessed summer's day,
  The flow'rets bloomed, the air was mild;
The little birds poured forth their lay,
  And everything in nature smiled.

In pleasant thought I wandered on
  Beneath the deep wood's ample shade,
Till suddenly I came upon
  Two children that had hither strayed.

Just at an aged birch tree's foot
  A little girl and boy reclined;
His hand in hers she kindly put,
  And then I saw the boy was blind.

"Dear Mary," said the poor blind boy,
  "That little bird sings very long;
Say, do you see him in his joy?
  And is he pretty as his song?"

"Yes, Edward, yes," replied the maid;
  "I see the bird on yonder tree:"

The poor boy sighed and gently said,
  "Sister, I wish that I could see!

"The flowers, you say, are very fair,
  And bright green leaves are on the trees,
And pretty birds are singing there:
  How beautiful for one who sees!

"Yet I the fragrant flowers can smell,
  And I can feel the green leaf's shade;
And I can hear the notes that swell
  From those dear birds that God has made.

"So, sister, he to me is kind,
  Though sight, alas! he has not given;
But tell me, are there any blind
  Among the children up in heaven?"

"No, dearest Edward, there, all see;
  But wherefore ask a thing so odd?"
"Oh, Mary, he's so good to me,
  I thought I'd like to look at God."

THE HEAVENLY FATHER.

WITHIN a town of Holland once
   A widow dwelt, 'tis said ;
So poor, alas ! her children asked
   One night in vain for bread ;
But this poor woman loved the Lord,
   And knew that he was good ;
So, with her little ones around,
   She prayed to him for food.
When prayer was done, her eldest child—
   A boy of eight years old—
Said softly, " In the Holy Book,
   Dear mother, we are told
How God, with food by ravens brought,
   Supplied his prophet's need."
" Yes," answered she, " but that, my son,
   Was long ago indeed !"

" But, mother, God may do again
   What he has done before !
And so, to let the birds fly in,
   I will unclose the door."

Then little Dirk, in simple faith,
  Threw open the door full wide,
So that the radiance of their lamp
  Fell on the path outside.

Ere long the burgomaster passed,
  And, noticing the light,
Paused to inquire why the door
  Was open so at night.
" My little Dirk has done it, sir,"
  The widow smiling said,
" That ravens might fly in, to bring
  My hungry children bread."

" Indeed !" the burgomaster cried ;
  " Then here's a raven, lad ;
" Come to my home and you shall see
  Where bread may soon be had."
Along the street to his own house
  ⚜ He quickly led the boy,
And sent him back with food, that filled
  This humble home with joy.

The supper ended, little Dirk
   Went to the open door,
Looked up and said, "Many thanks, good
     Lord!"
Then shut it fast once more;
For, though no bird had entered in,
   He knew that God on high
Had hearkened to his mother's prayers,
   And sent this full supply.

THE CHILDHOOD OF JESUS.

In the green fields of Palestine,
   By its fountains and its rills,
And by the flowing Jordan's stream,
   And o'er the vine-clad hills,

Once lived and roved the fairest child
   That ever blessed the earth—
The happiest and the holiest
   That e'er had human birth.

How beautiful his childhood was,
   Harmless and undefiled!
Oh dear to his young mother's heart
   Was this pure, sinless child.

Kindly in all his deeds and words,
   And gentle as the dove,
Obedient, affectionate,
   His very soul was love.

Oh, is it not a blessed thought,
   Children of human birth,
That once the Saviour was a child
   And lived upon the earth?

RINGING THE BELL,

OR DOING SOMETHING FOR GOD.

A MISSIONARY far away
   Beyond the Southern Sea,
Was sitting in the house one day,
   His Bible on his knee.

When suddenly he heard a rap
 Upon his chamber door;
And opening, there stood a boy
 Of some ten years or more.

"Dear sir!" he said in native tongue,
 "I do so want to know
If something for the house of God
 You'll kindly let me do?"

"What can you do, my little boy?"
 The missionary said,
And as he spoke he laid his hand
 Upon the youthful head.

Then bashfully, as if afraid
 His secret wish to tell,
The boy in eager accents said,
 "Oh let me ring the bell!"

"Oh please to let me ring the bell
 For our dear house of prayer;
I'm sure I'll ring it loud and well,
 And I'll be always there."

The missionary kindly spoke;
The boy had pleaded well,
And to the eager child he said,
"Yes, you shall ring the bell."

Oh what a joyful, happy heart
He carried to his home!
And how impatiently he longed
For the Sabbath-day to come!

He rang the bell, he went to school,
The Bible learned to read;
And in his youthful heart was sown
The gospel's precious seed.

And now to other heathen lands
He's gone, of Christ to tell;
And yet his first young mission was
To ring the Sabbath-bell.

THE LITTLE ANGEL.

RIGHT into our house one day
A dear little angel came;
I ran to him and said softly,
"Little angel, what is your name?"

11

He said not a word in answer,
 But he smiled a beautiful smile;
Then I said, " May I go home with you?
 Shall you go in a little while ?"

But mamma said, " Dear little angel,
 Don't leave us—oh always stay;
We will all of us love you dearly,
 Sweet angel—oh don't go away."

So he stayed, and he stayed, and we loved
  him
 As we could not have loved another;
" Do you want to know what his name is?
 His name is my little brother!"

READY FOR DUTY.

DAFFY-DOWN-DILLY came up in the cold,
 Through the brown mould;
Although the March breezes blew keen on
 her face,
Although the white snow lay on many a
 place,

Daffy-down-dilly had heard under ground
The sweet rushing sound
Of the streams, as they burst off their white
winter chains,
Of the whistling spring winds and the patter-
ing rains.

"Now, then," thought Daffy, deep down in
her heart,
"It's time I should start;"
So she pushed her soft leaves through the
hard frozen ground,
Quite up to the surface, and then she looked
round.

There was snow all about her, gray clouds
overhead,
The trees all looked dead;
Then how do you think Daffy-down-dilly
felt,
When the sun would not shine and the ice
would not melt?

"Cold weather!" thought Daffy, still working away;
"The earth's hard to-day;
There's but a half inch of my leaves to be
seen,
And two-thirds of that is more yellow than
green.

"I can't do much yet, but I'll do what I can;
It's well I began;
For unless I can manage to lift up my head,
The people will think that the Spring her-
self's dead."

So, little by little she brought her leaves out,
All clustered about;
And then her bright flowers began to unfold,
Till Daffy stood robed in her spring green
and gold.

Oh, Daffy-down-dilly, so brave and so true;
I wish all were like you;
So ready for duty in all sorts of weather,
And holding forth courage and beauty to-
gether.

MISS WARNER.

A CHILD'S DREAM OF HEAVEN.

DEAR MOTHER, I dreamed about heaven ;
  I stood at the pearly gate ;
I lifted my little hands to knock,
  But they did not let me wait.

It slowly swung on its golden hinge ;
  And I saw two angels stand,
Dressed in the softest, purest white,
  One upon either hand.

They held two beautiful harps, mother,
  Of shining glittering gold ;
Which one played the sweeter,
  I'm sure I could not have told.

And the song they sang was, "Welcome,
  Oh welcome, little child ;
Fear not to enter heaven's gate,
  Washed clean and undefiled."

And so I fearless walked inside,
  And oh it was lovelier far
Than any garden I ever saw ;
  Each flower shone like a star.
11 *

And the trees all rustled in music;
 Each leaf sang its little song;
It sounded like the church organ,
 Sweetly solemn and strong.

And I saw a beautiful fountain,
 That fell like rippling light;
Even the beams of the moon, mother,
 Are not so dazzlingly bright

Around it played little children;
 All looked happy and smiled;
I did not see an angry look
 On the face of any child.

And thus I wandered a long, long time;
 No unkind sound I heard;
They were gentle and sweet as sweet could be,
 And love was in every word.

I spoke to the little children,
 And asked "If I might stay,
Hearing the beautiful music,
 Watching the fountains play."

But they said, " The daylight cometh,
    When you must go back to earth ;
But, if you are good and gentle
    And innocent in your mirth ;

" If you do not strike your playmates,
    Or say an unkind word,
And put down the ugly feelings
    That may in your heart be stirred,

" Some time a beautiful angel,
    With wings of snowy. white,
Will bear you up in his powerful arms
    To our dear Lord's garden of light.

" And here you can stay for ever,
    In the garden of the Lord,
And bathe in the life-giving fountains
    According to his word."

And then I woke right up, mother ;
    But I'm going to try to be
All that the little children said,
    So that God may send for me.

JULIE LEONARD.

MOTHER'S LAST WORDS.

PART FIRST.

THE yellow fog lay thick and dim
   O'er London city, far and wide;
It filled the spacious parks and squares,
   Where noble lords and ladies ride.

It filled the streets, the shops were dark,
   The gas was burning through the day
The Monument was blotted out,
   And lost in gloom the river lay.

But thicker still, and darker far,
   The noisome smoke-cloud grimly fell
Amongst the narrow courts and lanes
   Where toiling people poorly dwell.

No sun above, no lofty sky,
   No breezy breath of living air,
The heavy, stagnant, stifling fog
   Crept here and there and everywhere.

Down seven steep and broken stairs
  Its chill, unwelcome way it found,
And darkened with a deeper gloom
  A low, damp chamber under ground.

A glimmering light was burning there
  Beside a woman on a bed—
A worn-out woman, ghastly pale—
  Departing to the peaceful dead.

Two little boys, in threadbare clothes,
  Stood, pale and trembling, by her side;
And listening to his mother's words,
  The younger of them sadly cried.

The elder boy shed not a tear,
  Nor stirred a moment from his place,
But with a corner of the sheet
  He wiped his mother's cold, damp face.

" Ah, John !" she said, " my own dear boy,
  You'll soon be in this world alone ;
But you must do the best you can,
  And be good children when I'm gone.

"And listen, John; before 'tis night
　　My weary spirit will be free;
　Then go and tell the overseer,
　　For he must come to bury me.

"You'll walk behind my coffin, dears;
　　There's little more I have to crave;
　But I should like to have my boys
　　Just drop a tear beside my grave.

"And then you'll have to leave this room,
　　Because the rent is not all paid;
　Since I've been ill I've let it run;
　　You know I've barely earned your bread.

"I don't owe much; I've minded that,
　　And paid it up, though hardly pressed;
　The man must take the little things,
　　And sell the bed to pay the rest.

"I've mended up your bits of clothes;
　　It is not much you've left to wear,
　But keep as decent as you can,
　　And don't neglect the house of prayer.

" I can't speak of your father, John;
    You know that he has been my death;
If he comes back you'll say his wife
    Forgave him with her dying breath.

" But oh, my children! when I'm gone,
    Do mind your mother's warning well,
And shun all drinking, swearing ways,
    As you would shun the pit of hell.

" I'm going to a happy place,
    So beautiful and dazzling bright;
'Twas in a vision or a dream
    It passed before me in the night.

" I felt my spirit caught away
    From all the crowd of toiling folk,
Above the cross upon St. Paul's,
    And far above the fog and smoke.

" And higher, higher up I went,
    Until I reached a golden gate,
Where all about in shining rows
    I saw the holy angels wait.

" At once they bade me welcome there,
    And all at once began to sing,
   'Come in, thou blessed of the Lord,
     For thou art welcome to the King.'

" Then one stepped forth, and took my hand,
    And spake like music, passing sweet :
   'We have been watching for thee long,
     To bring thee to our Master's feet.'

" Then, hand in hand, we floated on
    Through glowing fields of lovely flowers,
   And saw ten thousand happy souls
    At rest among the shining bowers.

" Our Saviour walked among them, John ;
    Most beautiful he was to see,
   And such a heavenly smile he gave
    When first he saw poor worthless me.

" And oh the gracious things he spoke,
    I hardly could believe the word ;
   'Come in, thou faithful one,' he said,
    'And rest thee now beside thy Lord.'

"Then all around I heard the sound
　　Of joyous voices singing praise,
And I stood there and joined the song,
　　And looked upon his blessed face.

" And as I looked my heart grew strong,
　　And then I fell before his feet;
' Dear Lord,' I said, ' I pray thee send
　　An angel to our wicked street.

" ' I've left two little boys behind,
　　To get through this bad world alone,
And much I fear they'll miss their way,
　　And never reach thy glorious throne.'

" ' I will,' he said; and then he called
　　A beauteous angel by his name,
And swifter than an arrow flies
　　That beauteous angel to him came.

" And as I knelt before his feet
　　I heard the order plainly given,
That he should guard my little boys
　　And bring them safe to me in heaven.
12

"I saw the angel bow his head
    And cast on me a look of love,
Then spread his snowy wings to leave
    His blissful seat in heaven above.

"So do not fret about my death;
    I know you'll not be left alone,
For God will send the angel down
    To care for you when I am gone.

"I'm sure you will have daily bread;
    For that the King gave strict command,
And all the wealth of London town
    Is in the power of his hand.

"So never join with wicked lads
    To steal, and swear, and drink, and lie;
For, though you are but orphans here,
    You'll have a Father in the sky.

"I can't see plain what you should do,
    But God, I think, will make your way;
So don't go to the workhouse, dears,
    But try for work, and always pray."

The woman ceased and closed her eyes,
  And long she lay as if at rest;
Then opened wide her feeble arms
  And clasped her children to her breast.

And then aloft her hands she raised,
  And heavenward gazed with beaming eyes:
"I see, I see, the angel come—
  I see him coming from the skies.

"Good-bye, good-bye, my children dear;
  My happy soul is caught away;
I hear, I hear my Saviour call—
  He calls me up, I cannot stay."

Then soared her soul from that dark room—
  Above the crowd of toiling folk,
Above the cross upon St. Paul's,
  Above the fog, above the smoke.

And higher, higher up she went,
  Until she saw the golden gate
Where night and day, in shining bands,
  The holy angels watch and wait.

And she went in and saw the King,
    And heard the gracious words he spoke
To her, who in this sinful world
    Had meekly borne her daily yoke.

But sadly sobbed the little boys.
    As from the bed of death they crept;
Upon the floor they sat them down,
    And long and piteously they wept.

The dreary walls around them closed;
    No father came to share their grief;
No friendly neighbor heard their cry,
    None came with pity or relief.

They cried until their tears were spent,
    And darker still the chamber grew;
And then said little Christopher,
    " Now, mother's dead, what shall we do?"

Then John rose up, and with his sleeve
    He wiped away the last sad tear:
" Well, we must go, as mother said,
    And tell the parish overseer."

" But won't the angel come to us ?"
  " I cannot tell you," John replied;
" I think he will," said Christopher;
  " My mother saw him when she died."

They stumbled up the broken stairs,
  And pushed their way along the street,
Whilst out of sight an angel bright
  Walked close behind with shining feet.

He stood beside them at the door,
  And heard the growling overseer;
Then touched his heart with sudden smart,
  And brought an unexpected tear.

" Here, lads," he said, " divide this bread;
  You both look hungry, any way;
We'll see about the body, child,
  And bury it on Wednesday."

The hungry children ate the loaf,
  And then the younger brother said,
" Our mother told us right, you see;
  That was all true about the bread."

12 *

"It does seem so," was John's reply;
　"I say, Chris, sha'n't you be afraid
To go and sleep at home to-night,
　All in the dark there with the dead?"

"Why should we, John?　Dead folks don't
　　hurt;
　She would not hurt us, if she could;
And as she laid upon the bed
　She looked so happy and so good!"

"Well, come down, then—I'm not afraid;"
　They entered in and shut the door,
And made a bed as best they could,
　And laid them down upon the floor.

And soundly slept those little boys,
　And dreamt about a far-off land,
With shining bowers and lovely flowers,
　And angels flying at command.

They'd never been beyond the town
　To see the beauteous works of God,
Not even seen the daisies spring
　By thousands on the level sod.

They had not seen a robin's nest,
    Nor plucked a violet in the shade,
Nor stood beside a running brook
    And heard the pleasant sound it made.

They had not seen young lambs at play,
    Nor gleaned among the autumn sheaves,
Nor listened to the pattering sound
    Of falling rain upon the leaves.

The cuckoo's note was strange to them;
    They'd never heard a wild bird sing,
Nor seen the yellow cowslip grow
    About the meadows in the spring.

Nor had they run with rosy boys
    At early morning to the school,
Nor spent the pleasant holidays
    In catching minnows in the pool.

Ah, no! and yet they were not left
    With naught but death and darkness
        there;
A minister of love was sent
    In answer to their mother's prayer.

But little thought those orphan boys,
    When to their wretched bed they crept,
That all the night an angel bright
    Would watch beside them as they slept.

When dimly dawned the light they rose;
    Chris looked around with chattering
        teeth;
The sheet was spread from foot to head;
    He knew his mother lay beneath.

" Let's go out to the pump and wash,
    As she would always have us do;
We'd better mind about her words,
    I think," said John; " Chris, what **say**
        you?"

" Let's go," said Chris; " besides, you know,
    We've got our breakfast now to find:"
They went out in the narrow street;
    The shining angel went behind.

A woman at the baker's shop,
    Who knew the children of the dead,
Was touched with pity as they passed,
    And gave them each a roll of bread.

" 'Tis true," said little Christopher;
    " You may be sure the angel's come;
She never gave us bread before—
    No, not the value of a crumb."

The next day, and the next to that,
    The promise of the King was kept,
And every night that angel bright
    Stood by to guard them as they slept.

On Wednesday the people came
    And took the woman's corpse away;
Two little mourners walked behind,
    And saw the grave wherein it lay.

Fast fell the tears upon their cheeks,
    When little Christy raised his eyes,
And said, " Oh, mother, how I wish
    I were with you above the skies!"

'Twas but a thought passed through his
        mind,
    When soft a whisper seemed to come,
" Be patient, little Christopher;
    You are not very far from home."

The minister said, "Dust unto dust;"
   And then the poor boys left the place—
Two friendless boys in London town,
   Oh was not theirs a hapless case?

They wandered up and down the streets,
   And then went home to sleep once more,
And in the morning left the room,
   And took the key and locked the door.

They found the landlord at his house,
   And said, "Please, sir, our mother's dead;
She could not pay up all the rent,
   And we have got to earn our bread.

"But please, sir, we have brought the key,
   And left some things upon the shelf;
And there's the blanket and the bed;
   My mother thought you'd pay yourself."

"And so she's gone," the landlord said,
   "And you are left to face the strife?
Well, I will say I never knew
   A better woman in my life.

" Of course I'll take the things, my boy,
    For right is right, and so I must;
But there's a shilling for you both :
    You'll find it hard to earn your crust."

They thanked the man and left the house;
    " I'll tell you what we'll do," said John;
" This shilling here will buy a broom;
    We'll sweep a crossing of our own.

" We won't go to the workhouse, Chris,
    But act like men and do our best;
Our mother said, ' A crust, well earned,
    Is sweeter than a pauper's feast.' "

" Oh yes ; we'll work like honest boys,
    And if our mother should look down,
She'd like to see us with a broom
    And with a crossing of our own."

Away they went with anxious hopes,
    And long they hunted here and there,
Until they found a dirty place
    Not very far from Leicester Square.

And here at once they took their stand,
　And swept a pathway broad and neat,
Where ladies in their silken gowns
　Might cross and hardly soil their feet.

The people hurried to and fro,
　And midst the jostle, jar and noise,
And thinking of their own affairs,
　They hardly saw the little boys.

Not so with all; some caught a sight
　Of little Christy's anxious eyes,
And put a penny in his cap,
　And every penny was a prize.

At last the streets began to clear,
　And people dropped off, one by one;
"Let's go," said little Christopher;
　"My pocket is quite heavy, John."

They counted up the pence with glee,
　And went away to buy some bread,
And had a little left to pay
　For lodging in a decent bed.

Next day John kept his crossing clean,
  Swept off the mud and left it dry,
And little Christy held his cap,
  But did not tease the passers-by.

And many a one a penny gave
  Who marked the pale child's modest way:
Thus they'd a shilling left in hand
  When they went home on Saturday.

The woman at the baker's shop,
  In kind remembrance of the dead,
Had found the boys a lodging-place
  Where they could have a decent bed.

"Let's go to church," said Christopher;
  "She'd be so glad to see us there;
You recollect she often said,
  'Boys, don't forget the house of prayer!'"

"We're very shabby," John replied,
  "And hardly fit for such a place;
But I will do the best I can
  To polish up my hands and face."

Clear rang the bells that Sabbath morn
  As they went briskly up the street;
And out of sight the angel bright
  Walked close behind with shining feet.

Some idle boys, who played about,
  Threw stones and mocked as they went in;
" Ay, let them mock away," said John:
  " We need not care for them a pin."

A lady watched them as they sat,
  And when the service all was done,
Said, " Do you go to Sunday-school?"
  " No, ma'am, but we should like," said
    John.

She told them both the place and time;
  They went that afternoon to school;
The boys were playing in the street,
  And said to John, " You are a fool—

" To go to that old stupid place;
  We know a trick worth two of that:"
Said John, " I mean to be a man,
  And that's the trick I'm aiming at."

PART SECOND.

THE second week was bleak and cold,
  A drizzling rain fell day by day,
And with their wet umbrellas up
  The people hurried on their way.

And no one thought about the boys,
  Who patiently stood sweeping there;
And sometimes over Christy's face
  There fell a shade of blank despair.

Discouraged, wet and weary oft,
  Cold, shivering to their bed they crept;
But still all night, that angel bright
  Stood by to guard them as they slept.

And these poor boys would sleep as well
  As rich men on their beds of down,
And wake up with a lighter heart
  Than many a king who wears a crown.

But winter-time came on apace,
  And colder still the weather grew,

And when they left the street at night
  Their clothes were often wet quite through.

Their coats were almost worn to rags,
  Their bare feet rested on the stones;
But still they always went to church,
  And to the school on afternoons.

And never joined with wicked boys,
. And never stopped away to play,
But tried to do their very best,
  And swept the crossing every day.

One day a boy came up and said,
  "I know a dodge worth two of that;
Just take to picking pockets, lad,
  And don't hold out that ragged hat."

"What, steal!" said little Christopher;
  "Our dodge is twice as good as that;
We earn our bread like honest folks;"
  And so he answered tit-for-tat.

"Well, that's your own lookout, of course;
  For my part, I don't see the fun

Of starving at this crossing here,
　When money is so easy won."

" How do you manage that ?" said John.
　"Oh ! come with us, we'll have you
　　　taught ;
　You've but a trick or two to learn—
　　To grip the things, and not be caught."

" But if you should be caught ?" said John,
　"The end of that would spoil your fun."
" Oh we know how to manage that ;
　Come on ! I'll show you how 'tis done."

" What do you get to eat ?" said John,
　Who pondered on these boasting words.
" What get to eat !—just what we choose—
　We eat and drink away like lords.

" Now, what d'ye say? Make up your mind ;
　I'm waited for, and must be gone,
We've pretty work to-day on hand."
　" Well, I sha'n't help to-day," said John.

13 *

"The more fool you," replied the boy,
    And went off whistling down the street;
And black as night a wicked sprite
    Went after him with rapid feet.

John went back slowly to his place,
    And grumbling to himself he said,
"I half repent I did not go,
    It is so hard to earn one's bread.

"I dare say he gets in a day
    As much as we earn in a week;
I wish I'd gone." John muttered this;
    To Christopher he did not speak.

At night, as he went sauntering home,
    He loitered round a pastry-cook's,
Till Christy called, "John, come along;
    You'll eat the cakes up with your looks!"

"Well, Chris, I say 'tis very hard
    We never have good things to eat;
I'm tired of eating just that bread;
    I long for something nice and sweet."

" They do look nice," said little Chris,
    And lingered near with hankering eyes;
" Which would you have, John, if you could?
    I'd have those jolly Christmas pies."

John answered in a grumbling tone,
    " Oh, I don't know, so let 'em be;
Some boys do get nice things to eat—
    Not honest boys like you and me."

" Well, never mind," said little Chris;
    " You're out of sorts this evening, John;
We'll both be rich maybe some day,
    And then we'll eat 'em up like fun."

" No chance of that for us," said John;
    " Our feet are now upon the stones;
We can't earn food and clothing too,
    And you are only skin and bones."

" 'Tis hard to work and not to eat;
    But, John, you would not do what's bad!"
" No, I don't mean to steal—not I—
    But when thieves feast it makes one mad."

And so John grumbled day by day,
  And longed for something good to eat,
And sometimes looked out for the boy
  Who went off whistling down the street.

And oh, indeed, 'twas very hard,
  When tired, hungry, cold and wet,
To pass by all the eating-shops
  That looked so tempting in the street;

To see the people going in
  To buy the puddings, cakes and pies,
Whilst they could only stand outside
  And look at them with longing eyes.

'Twas hard to see the smoking meat,
  And smell the vapors floating round
Of roasting joints and savoury steaks
  From steaming kitchens under ground.

And sometimes little Christy cried,
  When, limping on with chilblain'd toes,
He saw fine windows full of boots
  And children's shoes in shining rows.

But still he never would complain,
    And sometimes said, if John was sad,
" We got on bravely yesterday;
    Why should you take to moping, lad?

" But, John, I think if you and I
    Were rich, as these great people are,
We'd just look out for orphan boys
    And give them nice warm clothes to
        wear."

" Just so," said John, " and we would
        give
Poor little sweepers in the street
A famous lot of bright pennies,
    To buy them something good to eat.

" They'd never miss the little things
    That would make kings of me and
        you;
I wish that we were rich men, Chris,
    We'd show 'em what rich men should
        do."

PART THIRD.

One night, between the dark and light,
  As they were going down a lane,
And Christopher, with bleeding feet,
  Was slowly hobbling on with pain,

John saw some shoes outside a door:
" They're sure to keep poor Christy warm!"
And quick as thought he snatched them up
  And tucked them underneath his arm.

Then pale as ashes grew his face,
  And sudden fears rushed on his mind;
He hurried on with quicker pace,
  Lest some one should be close behind.

" Do stop a bit," his brother cried;
  " Don't be in such a hurry, John."
John darted round a frightened look,
  And from a walk began a run.

He thought he heard the cry of " Thief,"
  And swifter down the street he fled;
And black as night a wicked sprite
  With rapid feet behind him sped.

The cry of "Thief!" was in his ears
    Through all the bustle and the din;
And when he reached the lodging-house,
    The wicked spirit followed in.

He sat down pale and out of breath,
    And locked the door into the street,
And trembled when he only heard
    The sound of little Christy's feet.

"There, Christy, boy—there's shoes for you,
    And now you'll cut away like fun;
Come, let us see how well they fit—
    Just give a tug, and they'll be on."

Then Christopher did laugh outright,
    "Hurra! hurra!—now I am shod;
But, John, where did you get the shoes?"
    John put him off, and gave a nod.

The little boy was tired out,
    And quickly to his bed he crept,
And knew not that a wicked sprite
    Scowled on his brother as he slept.

John could not rest; the faintest noise
    Made all the flesh upon him creep;
He turned, and turned, and turned again,
    But could not get a wink of sleep.

He strained his ears to catch the sound
    Of footsteps in the silent night,
And when they came close by the door,
    His hair almost rose up with fright.

At last his fear became so great
    That in a cold, damp sweat he lay,
And then the thought came in his mind
    That he had better try and pray.

"They tell us at the Sunday-school,
    That we must beg to be forgiven:
My mother used to say the same
    Before she went away to heaven.

"I wish I'd let the shoes alone;
    I wonder what I'd better do?
If I should take them back again,
    Poor Christy would not have a shoe.

"Though I don't think he'd care for that,
   For he's a better boy than I,
And he would sooner starve to death
   Than steal a thing or tell a lie.

"Are you asleep, Chris? Can't you wake?
   I want to tell you something bad;
I've counted all the hours to-night;
   I say, Chris, can't you wake up, lad?"

Just then the child screamed in his sleep,
   And started upright in his bed:·
"Are you there, John? Who's in the room?
   Oh, John! I dreamt that you were dead.

"I'm glad enough that I woke up,
   I'm glad you're all alive and well;
I'd such an ugly dream—I saw
   The devil taking you to hell."

"And so he will, if I don't mind;
   As far as that, your dream is right;
And as to going off to hell,
   I think I've been in hell all night."

14

" What have you done?"   " Why, stole some
        shoes—
    That very pair I gave to you;
  But I can't rest about it, Chris;
    I want to know what we shall do.

" Why, take them back, of course," said Chris,
    " And put them where they were before;
  Let's go at once."   " No, stop," said John,
    " The clock has only just struck four.

" There's no one stirring in the street,
    The shops will not be opened yet,
  And we should have to wait about
    For hours in the cold and wet.

" And now, that I've made up my mind,
    I don't feel half so much afraid."
  Then took to flight that evil sprite,
    And John lay down his weary head.

  At six o'clock the boys went out;
    The snow was falling in the street;
  And through the bitter morning air
    They ran along with naked feet.

They watched the busy town wake up,
    Undoing shutter, bolt and bar;
But full two hours they walked about
    Before that door was set ajar.

John quickly slipped the shoes inside,
    And then as quickly walked away,
And with a lighter heart he went
    To face the labors of the day.

Fast fell the feathery, floating snow,
    In whirling currents driven round,
Or fluttered down in silent showers
    Of fleecy flakes upon the ground.

With broom in hand and shivering limbs
    The little sweepers bravely stood,
And faced the cutting north-east wind,
    That seemed to chill their very blood.

A lady, in a house close by,
    Who often watched the little boys,
Heard many times that stormy day
    A deep cough mingling with the noise.

She rose up from her blazing fire,
    And from the window looked about,
And hard at work amongst the snow
    She spied the ragged sweepers out.

" Do, Geraldine, look here," she said ;
    " How thin that youngest boy has grown !
Poor little wretch ! how cold he looks,
    He's little more than skin and bone."

" Poor little boy !" said Geraldine ;
    " I never saw a paler face ;
I think they must be honest boys,
    They keep so constant to their place.

" There's Frank's and Freddy's worn-out
        shoes,
    I think would fit them very well."
" Perhaps they would ; I'll have them brought,
    My dear, if you will ring the bell.

" And there's your brothers' old great coats,
    They'll never put them on again ;
But they would keep these children warm
    In many a storm of wind and rain."

Mother's Last Words.

" And give them something nice to eat;
  I don't mean dry old crusts of bread,
But good mince-pies," said Geraldine;
  " You know we have a plenty made."

" Well do so, if you like, my dear."
  " Oh, thank you ; they shall have some
    pies."
Poor John and little Christopher,
  They hardly could believe their eyes.

They took the clothes and nice mince-pies,
  They bowed and thanked, and bowed
    again,
Then scampered down the splashy streets,
  And reached their own dull, dirty lane.

And there they fitted on their coats,
  And turned the pockets inside out,
Stuck up the collars round their ears,
  Put on the shoes and marched about.

They rubbed their hands and laughed amain,
  And twisted one another round,
14 *

And then John turned a somerset,
And cleared the bedstead with a bound.

"But now for these fine Christmas pies,"
He said, and smacked his lips with
glee,
"They're just the things you wanted, Chris—
There's two for you and two for me.

"We never had such luck before,
We never dreamt of such a thing."
"I think 'twas mother's angel, John,
Who had that order from the King."

"You don't mean that in earnest, Chris?"
"Why not?" said Chris, "I'm sure I
do.
I say, John, if we died to-night,
Should we both go to heaven, too?"

"Well, Christopher, last night I thought
I should be sure to go to hell;
What sort of place that's like to be
I've now a notion I could tell.

"I'm pretty sure if I had died
　　Last night, without my sins forgiven,
I'd not a single chance to go
　　To be with mother up in heaven.

"I wish I'd never touched the shoes;
　.To steal is such a shameful sin,
And though they're taken back again,
　　I don't feel yet all right within.

"It was so bad to go and steal;
　　Four months to-day you know she died;
And though we've fared quite hard enough,
　　Our wants have mostly been supplied.

"Some boys, we know, have had no bed—
　　A deal worse off than you or I,
For we have always had some bread,
　　And just a place where we could lie.

"And now we've got some clothes to wear,
　　And days will soon be getting long,
And then, old boy, we'll shortly see
　　You picking up and getting strong."

'I don't know, John—I fancy not;
  'I sometimes think I'm going to die;
I dream so much about the place
  Where mother went—I don't know why,

"Except, maybe, I'm going too.
  I saw one night, John, in a doze,
That angel that my mother saw,
  With snowy wings and shining clothes.

"He looked at me, and then he smiled,
  And said, 'Your time will soon be come;
Be patient, little Christopher—
  You're going to a better home.'

"You know last Sunday at the school
  The lady told us how to pray,
And said, 'that Jesus Christ had come
  To die and take our sins away.'

"And so I begged he'd take all mine;
  And, Johnny, I believe he will;
And now I should not mind to die,
  If we could be together still."

" Oh, Christy, boy, you must not die;
  What should I do without you here?
Oh, do get well—you must get well,"
  And John brushed off a starting tear.

The winter passed, and spring-time came,
  And summer days grew warm and long,
But little Christy weaker grew,
  And soon could hardly creep along.

And then he stopped all day at home,
  And soon he hardly left his bed;
And John was forced to leave him there
  To earn for both their daily bread.

Sometimes the lady at the house
  Gave John some little jobs to do,
And when she found he did them well,
  She sent him on her errands too.

And now when Christopher was ill,
  And John was leaving for the night,
She gave him little dainty things
  To please his brother's appetite.

The woman at the baker's shop
   Had always been a faithful friend,
And often came to see the child,
   And stayed a while to wash and mend.

The lady at the Sunday-school
   Found out the little orphans' home,
And she would come and read to Chris,
   And he was glad to see her come.

She talked about the heavenly King,
   And she would kneel and softly pray;
And thus he lingered on a while,
   Still getting weaker day by day.

'Twas on a sultry summer's night,
   When heavy lay the stifling air,
As John was dropping off to sleep,
   He heard a softly-whispered prayer.

He knew 'twas Chris, and did not stir,
   And then he heard a gentle sigh;
It was the dear boy's happy soul
   Escaping to its home on high.

He left behind his wasted form ;
　He rose above the toiling folk,
Above the cross upon St. Paul's,
　Above the fog, above the smoke.

And higher, higher, up he went,
　Until he reached the golden gate,
Where night and day, in shining bands,
　The holy angels watch and wait.

And he went in and saw the King,
　The Saviour who for him had died,
And found once more his mother dear ;
　And little Chris was satisfied.

And there they both together wait
　Till John shall reach that happy home,
And often from the golden gate
　They watch in hopes to see him come.

But John had many years to live,
　For he had useful work to do ;
And he grew up an honest man,
　A sober man, and Christian too.

His friend, the lady at the house,
　When little Chris was dead and gone,
Bound John apprentice to a trade,
　And so he did not feel alone.

And that bright minister of love,
　Appointed by the Saviour King
To guard those orphan boys on earth,
　And then to heavenly glory bring,

Still walked with John his journey through,
　And though unseen was ever nigh;
Nor left him till his work was done,
　And then went up with him on high.

And there, in everlasting joy,
　The mother and the brothers meet,
To part no more, and weep no more,
　Nor dwell in that dark, dirty street;

To toil no more with bleeding feet,
　Nor hungering long for something nice;
For they are clothed as angels are,
　And eat the fruits of Paradise.

No more the cold shall freeze their limbs,
 Nor darkness chill their dreary night;
It is eternal summer there,
 And all the blessed rest in light;

And there, with thousand thousand souls,
 All saved from sorrow, fear and shame,
They join to sing the happy song
 Of praise to God and to the Lamb.

Dear boys, who read the simple tale
 Of these poor sweepers in the street,
The gracious God who cared for them
 Will also guide your willing feet.

WHO SHALL STAND IN THE HOLY PLACE?

Oh who before the righteous God
 Shall uncondemned appear?
The man whose soul abides in truth,
 In deed and thought sincere;

The man whose heart from guile is pure,
 Whose hands from bribes are free;

15

Who honest poverty prefers
    To gainful perjury;

The man who to his plighted word
    Has ever firmly stood;
Who, though he promise to his hurt,
    Still makes his promise good;

Who throws the chambers of his soul
    Wide open to the light,
And strives each day and hour to live
    As in his Maker's sight.

EVERY DAY

SONGS AND BALLADS.

EVERY-DAY
SONGS AND BALLADS.

THE LITTLE DOVES.

High on the top of an old pine tree
Broods a mother dove, with her young ones
    three;
Warm over them is her soft downy breast,
And they sing so sweetly in their nest:
Coo! say the little ones—Coo! says she,
All in their nest in the old pine tree.

Soundly they sleep through the moonshiny
    night,
Each young one covered and tucked in tight;
Morn wakes them up with the first blush of
    light,
And they sing to each other with all their
    might:

15 *

Coo! say the little ones—Coo! says she,
All in their nest in the old pine tree.

When in their nest they are left all alone,
While their mother far for their dinner has
　　flown,
Quiet and gentle they all remain,
Till their mother they see come home again;
Then Coo! say the little ones—Coo! says she,
All in their nest in the old pine tree.

When they are fed by their tender mother,
One never will push nor crowd another;
Each opens wide his own little bill,
And he patiently waits and gets his fill;
Then Coo! say the little ones—Coo! says she,
All in their nest in the old pine tree.

Wisely the mother begins by and by
To make her young ones learn to fly,
Just for a little way over the brink,
Then back to the nest as quick as a wink;
And Coo! say the little ones—Coo! says she,
All in their nest in the old pine tree.

Fast grow the young ones, day and night,
Till their wings are plumed for a longer
　　flight;
Till unto them at the last draws nigh
The time when they all must say good-bye;
Then Coo! say the little ones—Coo! says she,
And away they fly from the old pine tree.

J. R.

MY LITTLE LAMMIE.

A NURSERY SONG.

As I walked over the hills one day,
I listened and heard a mother-sheep say:
" In all the green world, there is nothing so
　　sweet
As my little lammie, with his nimble feet;
With his eye so bright and his wool so white,
Oh he is my darling, my heart's delight.
The robin, he that sings in the tree,
Dearly may dote on his darlings four;
But I love my one little lambkin more."
And the mother-sheep and her little one
Side by side lay down in the sun,

And they went to sleep on the hill-side warm;
While *my little lammie* lies here on my arm.

I went into the kitchen, and what did I see
But the old gray cat and her kittens three?
I heard her whispering soft.   Said she,
"My kittens, with tails all so cunningly curled,
Are the prettiest things that can be in the
      world;
The bird on the tree, and the old ewe she,
May love their babies exceedingly,
But I love my kittens there, under the rock-
      ing-chair;

I love my kittens with all my might;
I love them at morning and noon and night;
Which is the prettiest I cannot tell—
Which of the three, for the life of me,
I love them all so well;
Now I'll take up my kitties, the kitties I
      love,
And we'll lie down together beneath the
      warm stove."
Let the kitties sleep under the stove so warm,
While *my little darling* lies here on my arm.

I went to the yard, and I saw the old hen
Go clucking about with her children ten.
She clucked and she scratched and she bristled
    away,
And what do you think I heard her say?
I heard her say, "The sun never did shine
On anything like to these chickens of mine;
You may hunt the full moon and the stars,
    if you please,
But you never will find ten such chickens as
    these;
The cat loves her kittens, the ewe loves her
    lamb,
But they do not know what a proud mother
    I am;
For lambs, nor for kittens, I won't part with
    these,
Though the sheep and the cat should go down
    on their knees;
No, no! not though the kittens should crow,
Or the lammie on two yellow legs could go;
My dear downy darlings, my sweet little
    things;
Come nestle now cozily under my wings;"

So the hen said, and the chickens all sped
As fast as they could to their nice feather
　　　bed ;
And there let them sleep in their feathers so
　　　warm,
While *my little chick* lies here on my arm.
LITTELL'S LIVING AGE.

MARY DOW.

COME in, little stranger, I said,
　　As she tapped at my half-open door,
While the blanket pinned over her head
　　Just reached to the basket she bore.

A look full of innocence fell
　　From her modest and pretty blue eye,
As she said, " I have matches to sell,
　　And hope you are willing to buy !

" A penny a bunch is the price ;
　　I think you will not find it too much ;
They're tied up so even and nice,
　　And ready to light with a touch."

I asked, " What's your name, little girl ?"
"'Tis Mary," she said—" Mary Dow !"
And carelessly tossed off a curl
    That played o'er her delicate brow.

" My father was lost in the deep,
    The ship never got to the shore ;
And mother is sad, and will weep
    When she hears the wind blow, and
      sea roar !

" She sits there at home without food,
    Beside our poor sick Willie's bed ;
She paid all her money for wood,
    And so I sell matches for bread.

" Every time that my dear mother tries
    Some things she'll get pay for to make,
And lays down the baby, it cries ;
    And that makes my sick brother wake.

" I go to the school, where I'm taught
    Of the Saviour so wise and so good,
Who knows every action and thought,
    And gives even ravens their food.

"And He, I am sure, who doth take
  Such fatherly care of a bird,
Will never forget or forsake
  His children who trust in his word.

"And now, if I only can sell
  The matches I brought out to-day,
I think I shall do very well,
  And mamma will rejoice at the pay."

Fly home, little bird, then I thought—
  Fly home full of joy to your nest;
For I took all the matches she brought,
  And Mary may tell you the rest.

THE SQUIRREL

A SQUIRREL sat on the topmost limb
Of a fine old hickory, graceful and slim;
For his breakfast he'd run over heather and
      heath,
And now he sat cozily picking his teeth.

And there as he sat, gently fanned by the breeze
That rustled the leaves of the old forest trees,

A poor wounded dove came and perched by
    his side,
And to his "good-morning" thus trembling
    replied :

" I warn you, Sir Squirrel, to run for your life,
Lest sorrow you bring on your children and
    wife ;
A hunter is coming with dog and with gun ;
As a friend, I advise you, Sir Squirrel, to run.

"Take warning, I pray, from my own bleeding
    breast,
And hasten away to your leaf-guarded nest !"
" Pooh, pooh !" said the squirrel, " I scorn thus
    to run ;
I fear not the hunter, his dog nor his gun !"

" Good-bye, then, Sir Squirrel, before it's too
    late ;
I go, and I leave you alone to your fate ;"
And away sped the dove over heather and
    heath,
But the squirrel sat cozily picking his teeth. .

16

When on came the hunter with dog and with
  gun,
And then the poor squirrel would gladly
  have run ;
But a victim he fell to his folly and pride,
And for scorning good counsel the poor squirrel died !

————◆◇◆————

THE BOY WHO NEVER TELLS A LIE.

Once there was a little boy,
  With curly hair and pleasant eye—
A boy who always told the truth,
  And never, never told a lie !

And when he trotted off to school,
  The children all about would cry,
" There goes the curly-headed boy,
  Who never, never tells a lie."

And everybody trusted him
  Because he always told the truth ;
And more and more, as he grew up,
  They loved the true and honest youth !

God is a God of truth, and when
 His little honest children die,
He takes them up to live with him,
 Where none can go who love " to lie!"

———◦◦◦———

THE DRUMMER-BOY'S BURIAL.

ALL day long the storm of battle
 Through the startled valley swept;
All night long the stars in heaven,
 O'er the slain sad vigils kept;
Oh the ghastly, upturned faces
 Gleaming whitely through the night!
Oh the heaps of mangled corses
 In that dim, sepulchral light!

One by one the pale stars faded,
 And at length the morning broke,
But not one of all the sleepers
 On that field of death awoke;
Slowly passed the golden hours
 Of the long, bright summer day;
And upon that field of carnage
 Still the dead unburied lay,—

Lay there stark and cold, but pleading
　　With a dumb, unceasing prayer
For a little dust to hide them
　　From the staring sun and air;
But the foemen held possession
　　Of that hard-won battle-plain,
In unholy wrath denying
　　Even burial to our slain.

Once again the night closed o'er them—
　　Night so holy and so calm,
That the moonbeams hushed the spirit
　　Like the sound of prayer or psalm;
On a couch of trampled grasses,
　　Just apart from all the rest,
Lay a fair young boy, with small hands
　　Meekly folded on his breast.

Death had touched him very gently,
　　And he lay as if asleep;
Even his mother scarce had shuddered
　　At that slumber calm and deep;
For a smile of wondrous sweetness
　　Lent a radiance to the face,

And the hand of cunning sculptor
   Could have added naught of grace
To the marble limbs so perfect
   In their passionless repose,
Robbed of all save matchless pureness
   By the hard, unpitying foes;
And the broken drum beside him
   All his life's short story told—
How he did his duty bravely
   Till the death-tide o'er him rolled.

Midnight came with ebon garments
   And a diadem of stars,
While right upward in the zenith
   Hung the fiery planet Mars;
Hark! a sound of stealthy footsteps
   And of voices whispering low;
Was it nothing but the young leaves,
   Or the brooklet's murmuring flow?

Clinging closely to each other,
   Striving never to look round,
As they passed with silent shudder
   The pale corses on the ground,
16 *

Came two little maidens, sisters,
　　With a light and hasty tread,
And a look upon their faces
　　Half of sorrow, half of dread.

But they did not pause nor falter
　　Till with throbbing hearts they stood
Where the drummer-boy was lying
　　In that partial solitude;
They had brought some simple garments
　　From their wardrobes' scanty store;
And two heavy iron shovels
　　In their slender hands they bore.

Then they quickly knelt beside him,
　　Crushing back the pitying tears,
For they had no time for weeping
　　Nor for any girlish fears.
And they robed the icy body in its hour
　　of sorest need,
And they felt that death was holy, and
　　it sanctified the deed.

But they smiled and kissed each other
　　When their new, strange task was o'er;

And the form that lay before them
　　Its unwonted garments wore ;
Then with slow and weary labor
　　A small grave they hollowed out,
And they lined it with the withered
　　Grass and leaves that lay about ;
But the day was slowly breaking
　　Ere their holy work was done,
And in crimson pomp the morning
　　Heralded again the sun ;
Then those tender little maidens—
　　They were children of our foes—
Laid the body of our drummer-
　　Boy to undisturbed repose.

BOB-O'-LINK.

MERRILY swinging on brier and weed,
　　Near to the nest of his little dame,
Over the mountain-side or mead,
　　Robert of Lincoln is telling his name :
Bob-o'-link, bob-o'-link—spink, spank, spink !
　　Snug and safe is that nest of ours,
Hidden among the summer flowers—chee,
　　　　chee, chee !

Robert of Lincoln is gayly drest,
　Wearing a bright black wedding-coat ;
White are his shoulders and white his crest ;
　Hear him call in his merry note—
Bob-o'-link, bob-'o-link—spink, spank, spink !
　Look what a nice new coat is mine,
Sure there was never a bird so fine—chee,
　　chee, chee !

Robert of Lincoln's Quaker wife,
　Pretty and quiet, with plain brown wings,
Passing at home a patient life,
　Broods in the grass while her husband
　　sings,
Bob-o'-link, bob-o'-link—spink, spank, spink !
　Brood, kind creature, you need not fear
Thieves and robbers while I am here—chee,
　　chee, chee !

Modest and shy as a nun is she,
　One weak chirp is her only note ;
Braggart, and prince of braggarts, is he,
　Pouring boasts from his little throat—
" Never was I afraid of man ;
Catch me cowardly knaves, if you can !"

Six white eggs on a bed of hay,
  Flecked with purple, a pretty sight;
There, as the mother sits all day,
  Robert is singing with all his might—
"Nice good wife, that never goes out,
Keeping house while I frolic about!"

Soon as the little ones chip the shell
  Six wide mouths are open for food;
Robert of Lincoln bestirs him well,
  Gathering seeds for the hungry brood—
"This new life is likely to be
Hard for a young fellow like me."

Robert of Lincoln at length is made
  Sober with work and silent with care;
Off is his holiday garment laid,
  Half forgotten that merry air—
"Nobody knows but my mate and I
Where our nest and nestlings lie."

Summer wanes—the children are grown;
  Fun and frolic no more he knows;

Robert of Lincoln's a humdrum crone;
   Off he flies and we sing as he goes—
"When you can pipe that merry old strain,
Robert of Lincoln, come back again !"
W. C. BRYANT.

POOR MAMMA.

DEAR MOTHER, get my bonnet, do!
   I want to go and play;
And, mother, hurry, tie my shoe,
   Or puss will run away;
And please, mamma, untie this string,
   It's in a hateful knot;
And tell me where I put my sling—
   I really have forgot.

Mamma, said Jane, my dress is loose,
   I wish you'd hook it up;
Oh dear! I want a drink so bad,
   But I can't reach the cup.
Mamma, cries John, I want a string
   To make my kite fly high,
And lots of paper for the tail,
   To make it reach the sky!

I've cut my finger, whimpers Pet,
    Do tie a rag upon it,
And, mamma, please sew this string
    Once more upon my bonnet;
And please comb out my tangled hair,
    And wash my face all clean,
For the children all are going to walk,
    And I'm not fit to be seen!

Mamma, where is my jumping-rope?
    Where did I put my hat?
I wish you'd help me build this house!
    Mamma, Bess plagues my cat!
Mamma, cries Dick, please tie my hoop,
    And draw a house for me;
And all the pictures in that book,
    Mamma, please show to me!

Now, every hour and every day
    Don't call mamma for aid;
But help yourself, and you'll help her,
    My darling little maid;
You, sir! don't be a thoughtless boy,
    But a thoughtful little man;

Play without help; put up each toy—
Help mamma all you can!

———•◦•———

GOOD-MORNING.

"Oh I am so happy!" a little girl said,
As she sprang like a lark from her low trun-
    dle bed;
"'Tis morning, bright morning, good-morn-
    ing, papa!
Just give me a kiss for good-morning, mamma:
Only just look at my pretty canary,
Chirping his sweet good-morning to Mary!
The sun is peeping straight into my eyes—
Good-morning to you, Mr. Sun, for you rise
Early to wake up my birdie and me,
And make us as happy as happy can be."

"Happy you may be, my dear little girl,"
And her mother stroked softly a clustering
    curl—
"Happy you may be, but think of the One
Who waked this morning both you and the
    sun!"

The little girl turned her bright eyes with a
    nod :
" Mamma, may I say good-morning to God?"
" Yes, little darling one, surely you may ;
Kneel as you kneel every morning to pray."
Mary knelt solemnly down, with her eyes
Looking up earnestly into the skies.

Two little hands that were folded together
Softly she laid on the lap of her mother.
" Good-morning, dear Father in heaven," she
    said ;
" I thank you for watching my snug little bed,
And for taking good care of me all the dark
    night,
And for waking me up with the beautiful
    light.
Oh keep me from naughtiness all the long day,
Dear Saviour, who taught little children to
    pray."

17

THE SPIDER AND THE FLY.

"WILL you walk into my parlor?" said the
    spider to the fly;
"'Tis the prettiest little parlor that ever you
    did spy;
The way into my parlor is up a winding
    stair,
And I have many pretty things to show you
    when you're there."

"Oh, no, no," said the little fly; "to ask me
    is in vain,
For who goes up your winding stairs can
    ne'er come down again."

"I'm sure you must be weary, dear, with
    soaring up so high;
Will you rest upon my little bed?" said the
    spider to the fly,
"There are pretty curtains drawn around, the
    sheets are fine and thin,
And if you like to rest a while, I'll snugly
    tuck you in."

"Oh, no, no," said the little fly, "for I've
    often heard it said,
They never, never wake again who sleep upon
    your bed.'

Said the cunning spider to the fly: "Dear
    friend, what can I do
To prove the warm affection I've always felt
    for you?
I have within my pantry good store of all
    that's nice;
I'm sure you're very welcome—will you please
    to take a slice?"

"Oh, no, no," said the little fly; "kind sir,
    that cannot be;
I've heard what's in your pantry, and I do
    not wish to see."

"Sweet creature," said the spider, "you're
    witty and you're wise;
How handsome are your gauzy wings, how
    brilliant are your eyes!

I have a little looking-glass upon my parlor
 shelf;
If you'll step in one moment, dear, you shall
 behold yourself."

" I thank you, gentle sir," she said, " for what
 you please to say,
And, bidding you good-morning now, I'll call
 another day."

The spider turned him round about and went
 into his den,
For well he knew the silly fly would soon
 come back again :
So he wove a subtle web in a little corner sly,
And set his table ready to dine upon the fly.

Then came he to his door again, and merrily
 did sing,
" Come hither, hither, pretty fly, with the
 pearl-and-silver wing ;
Your robes are green and purple, there's a
 crest upon your head ;
Your eyes are like the diamond, while mine
 are dull as lead."

Alas! alas! how very soon this silly little fly,
Hearing his wily, flattering words, came slowly
    flitting by!
With buzzing wings she hung aloft, then near
    and nearer drew,
Thinking only of her brilliant eyes and her
    green-and-purple hue;
Thinking only of her crested head, poor
    foolish thing! at last
Up jumped the cunning spider and fiercely
    held her fast;
He dragged her up his winding stair, into his
    dismal den,
Within his little parlor, but she ne'er came
    out again.

And now, dear little children who may this
    story read,
To idle, silly, flattering words I pray you ne'er
    give heed;
Unto all evil counselors close heart and ear
    and eye,
And take a lesson from this tale of the Spider
    and the Fly.

MARY HOWITT.

17 *

THE SNOW-BIRD.

THE ground was all covered with snow one
day,
And two little sisters were busy at play,
When a snow-bird was sitting close by, on a
tree,
And merrily singing his chick-a-dee-dee.

He had not been singing that tune very long,
Ere Emily heard him, so loud was his song;
"Oh, sister, look out of the window!" said she,
"Here's a dear little bird singing chick-a-
dee-dee.

"Poor fellow! he walks in the snow and the
sleet,
And has neither stockings nor shoes on his
feet;
I pity him so, how cold he must be!
And yet he keeps singing his chick-a-dee-dee.

"If I were a barefooted snow-bird, I know
I would not stay out in the cold and the
snow;

I wonder what makes him so full of his glee?
He's all the time singing that chick-a-dee-dee.

" Oh, mother, do get him some stockings and
    shoes,
And a nice little frock, and a hat if you
    choose ;
I wish he'd come into the parlor and see
How warm we would make him, poor chick-
    a-dee-dee !"

The bird had flown down for some pieces of
    bread,
And heard every word little Emily said.
" What a figure I'd make in that dress !"
    thought he,
And he laughed as he warbled his chick-a-
    dee-dee.

" I'm grateful," said he, " for the wish you
    express,
But I have no occasion for such a fine dress ;
I had rather remain with my little legs free,
Than be hobbling along, singing chick-a-
    dee-dee.

"There is one, my dear child, though I cannot
    tell who,
Has clothed me already, and warm enough too;
Good-morning! oh who are so happy as we?"
And away he flew, singing his chick-a-dee-dee.

WORDSWORTH.

<hr>

THE STOLEN NEST.

To-whit, to-whit, to-whee! will you listen to
    me?
Who stole four eggs I laid, and the nice nest
    I made?

Not I! said the cow, moo-oo—such a thing I
    never do;
I gave you a whisp of hay, but didn't take
    your nest away,
Not I! said the cow, moo-oo—such a thing I'd
    never do!

To-whit, to-whit, to-whee! will you listen to
    me?
Who stole four eggs I laid, and the nice nest
    I made?

Bob-o'-link, bob-o'-link, now what do you
    think—
Who stole a nest away from the plum tree to-
    day?

Not I! said the dog, bow-wow—I wouldn't be
    so mean, I know;
I gave hairs the nest to make, but the nest I
    did not take ;
Not I! said the dog, bow-wow—I wouldn't be
    so mean, I know!

Coo-coo, coo-coo, coo-coo! let me speak a
    word or two;
Who stole that pretty nest from little yellow-
    breast?

Not I, said the sheep; oh no, I wouldn't
    treat a poor bird so?
I gave wool the nest to line, but the nest is
    none of mine,
Baa, baa! said the sheep; oh no, I wouldn't
    treat a birdie so.

Caw, caw! said the crow—I should like to know
What thief took away a bird's nest to-day?

Cluck, cluck! said the hen, don't ask me
    again;
Why I haven't a chick would do such a
    trick;
We all gave her a feather, and she wove them
    together:
I would scorn to intrude upon her and her
    brood;
Cluck, cluck! said the hen—don't ask me
    again!

Chirr-a-whirr, chirr-a-whirr!
We will make a great stir;
Let us find out his name, and all cry, "For
    shame!"

To-whit, to-whit, to-whee! will you listen to
    me?
Who stole four eggs I laid, and the pretty
    nest I made?
Bob-o'-link bob-o'-link! now what do you
    think—
Who stole a nest away from the plum tree to-
    day?

Coo-coo, coo-coo, coo-coo ! let me speak a word
    or two ;
Who stole that pretty nest from little yellow-
    breast ?
Caw, caw ! cried the crow—I should like to
    know
What thief took away a bird's nest to-day ?
Chirr-a-whirr, chirr-a-whirr ! we will make a
    great stir ;
Let us find out his name, and all cry, " For
    shame !"

I would not rob a bird, said little Mary Green ;
I think I never heard of anything so mean !
'Tis very cruel too, said little Alice Neal ;
I wonder if he knew how sad the bird would
    feel ?

A little boy hung down his head,
And went and hid behind the bed,
For he stole that pretty nest
From little yellow-breast ;
And he felt so full of shame
He did not like to tell his name.
LITTLE SONGS FOR LITTLE PEOPLE.

MY LITTLE SISTER.

I HAVE a little sister; she's only two years old,
But she is a little darling, and worth her
weight in gold,
She often runs to kiss me when I'm at work
or play,
Twining her arms around me in such a pretty
way.

And then she says so sweetly, in innocence
and joy,
"Tell me a story, sister, about a little boy."
But sometimes when I'm knitting, she pulls
my needles out,
And then she skips and dances round with
such a merry shout.
It makes me laugh to see her, though I'm not
very glad
To have her take my needles out and make
my work so bad;
But I know if I would have her be sorry for
what she's done,
I must be very gentle when I tell her it is
wrong.

MINUTES AND YEARS.

SIXTY seconds make a minute!
Sixty minutes make an hour!
Twenty-four hours make a day,
Long enough for sleep and play.
In every month the weeks are four,
   And twelve whole months will make a year!
And when you are four, or a little more,
   You must work as well as play, my dear.

TUMBLE

TUMBLE up, tumble down, never mind it, my
    sweet!
No, no! never beat the poor floor;
'Twas your fault that you could not stand
    straight on your feet;
Beat yourself, if you beat any more.

Hush, hush! what a noise! Will a noise make
    it well?
Will crying wash bruises away?

18

Suppose it should bleed a little and swell?
It will all be gone down in a day.

That's right, be a man and dry up your tears;
  Come, smile now and give me a kiss;
If you live in the world but a very few years,
  You will have greater troubles than this.

JANE TAYLOR.

WHAT I HATE.

I HATE to see a little girl who does not love
    to rise,
Or have the water fresh and sweet cover her
    face and eyes;
I hate to see her clean smooth dress look
    wrinkled, tumbled, tossed,
Her toys all scattered here and there, her
    thread and needle lost.

I hate to see her at her play, when little girls
    are met
To frolic, laugh and run about, grow peevish,
    cry and fret;

I hate to hear her tell a lie, what is not hers
to take,
Mamma's commands to disobey, or papa's
rules to break.

WHAT I LOVE.

I love to see a little girl rise with the lark so
bright,
Bathe, comb and dress with pleasant face,
then thank God for the light;
And when she comes to meet mamma, so fresh
and neat and clean,
To kiss her and her dear papa with gentle,
modest mien.

I like to see her kindly play when little girls
are met,
And let the others have their way, and never
sulk or fret;
And never, never tell a lie, and nothing ever
take
That is not hers; and do all this for her dear
Saviour's sake.

BIRD'S NEST.

A LITTLE bird built a warm nest in a tree,
And laid some blue eggs in it—one, two, three;
And then very glad and delighted was she.

And after a while, but how long I can't tell,
The little ones crept one by one from their
    shell,
And the mother was pleased, for she loved
    them all well.

She spread her soft wings o'er them all the
    day long,
To warm them and guard them, her love was
    so strong;
And her mate sat beside her and sung her a
    song.

One day the young birds were all crying for
    food;
So off flew their mother, away from her brood,
And there came some boys who were wicked
    and rude.

They pulled the warm nest down, away from
    the tree;
The little ones cried, but they could not get
    free;
So at last they all died away—one, two, three.

When back to the nest the poor mother did
    fly,
Oh then she set up a most piteous cry;
And she mourned a long while, then lay
    down to die.

SONGS FOR THE LITTLE ONES AT HOME.

———◆——

THE BATH.

I LOVE the good splashing and plunging and
    dashing;
    Hurrah! the cold water for me!
I never will cry nor halloo; no, not I:
    Unless it's for joy and for glee;
Hurrah for a splash—come give me a dash;
    I don't care a fig for the cold;
It makes me so bright, so active and light,
    It's better than silver and gold.

18 *

PUSSY-CAT.

Pussy-cat lives in the servants' hall,
  She can set up her back and purr;
The little mice live in a crack in the wall,
  But they hardly dare venture to stir;

For whenever they think of taking the air,
  Or filling their little maws,
The pussy-cat says, Come out if you dare;
  I will catch you all with my claws.

Scrabble, scrabble, scrabble, went all the little
      mice,
  For they smelt the Cheshire cheese;
The pussy-cat said, It smells very nice;
  Now do come out if you please.

Squeak, said the little mouse—squeak, squeak,
      squeak,
  Said all the little ones too;
We never creep out when cats are about,
  Because we're afraid of you.

So the cunning old cat lay down on a mat
    By the fire in the servants' hall;
"If the little mice peep, they'll think I'm
      asleep;"
So she rolled herself up in a ball.

Squeak, said the little mouse, we'll creep out
    And eat some Cheshire cheese;
That silly old cat is asleep on a mat,
    And we may sup at our ease.

Nibble, nibble, nibble, went the little mice,
    And they licked their little paws;
Then the cunning old cat sprang up from the
      mat,
    And caught them all with her claws.

AUNT EFFIE.

THE GRAY SWAN.

"Oh tell me, sailor, tell me true—
Is my little lad, my Elihu,
    A sailing with your ship?"
The sailor's eyes were dim with dew—
"Your little lad, your Elihu?"

He said with trembling lip :
" What little lad ?—What ship ?

" What little lad ? as if there could be
Another such a one as he ;
   What little lad, do you say ?
Why Elihu, that took to the sea
The moment I put him off my knee ;
   It was just the other day
   The ' Gray Swan' sailed away."

" The other day !"—the sailor's eyes
Stood open with a great surprise.
   " The other day !—the Swan !"
His heart began in his throat to rise ;
" Ay, ay, sir ; here in the cupboard lies
   The jacket he had on !"
   " And so your lad is gone ?"

" Gone with the Swan ?" " And did she stand
With her anchor clutching hold of the sand
   For a month, and never stir ?"
" Why to be sure ; I've seen from the land,
Like a lover kissing his lady's hand,
   The wild sea kissing her !—
   A sight to remember, sir !"

" But, my good mother, do you know
All this was twenty years ago ?—
   I stood on the Gray Swan's deck,
And to that lad I saw you throw
Taking it off, as it might be so,
   The kerchief from your neck."
" Ay, and he'll bring it back."

" And did the little lawless lad
That has made you sick and made you sad,
   Sail with the Gray Swan's crew ?"
" Lawless !—the man is going mad,
The best boy ever mother had ;
   Be sure, he sailed with the crew—
What would you have him do ?"

" And he has never written a line,
Nor sent you word nor made you sign
   To say he was alive ?"
" Hold ! if 'twas wrong, the wrong is mine ;
Besides, he may be in the brine !
   And could he write from the grave ?
Tut, man ! what would you have ?"

"Gone twenty years—a long, long cruise—
'Twas wicked thus your love to abuse!
   But if the lad still live
And come back home, think you you can
Forgive him?"—"Miserable man!
   You're mad as the sea! you rave!
   What have I to forgive!"

The sailor twitched his shirt so blue,
And from within his bosom drew
   The kerchief—she was wild.
"O God, my Father, is it true,
My little lad! my Elihu!
   My blessed boy! my child!
   My dead—my living child?"

ALICE CAREY.

WE ARE SEVEN!

I MET a little cottage girl;
   She was eight years old, she said;
Her hair was thick with many a curl
   That clustered around her head,

"Sisters and brothers, little maid,
   How many may you be?"
"How many? Seven in all," she said,
   And wondering looked at me.

"And where are they? I pray you tell!"
   She answered, "Seven are we,
And two of us in Conway dwell,
   And two are gone to sea.

"Two of us in the churchyard lie,
   My sister and my brother,
And in the churchyard cottage I
   Dwell near them with my mother."

"You say that two at Conway dwell,
   ·And two are gone to sea,
Yet you are seven! I pray you tell
   Sweet maid, how this may be?"

Then did the little maid reply,
   "Seven boys and girls are we;
Two of us in the churchyard lie
   Beneath the churchyard tree!"

"You run about, my little maid,
   Your limbs, they are alive;
If two are in the churchyard laid,
   Then ye are only five!"

"Their graves are green; they may be seen,"
   The little maid replied,
"Twelve steps or more from mother's door,
   And they are side by side.

"My stockings there, I often knit,
   My kerchief there I hem,
And there upon the ground I sit—
   I sit and sing to them.

"And often after sunset, sir,
   When it is light and fair,
I take my little porringer
   And eat my supper there.

"The first that died was little Jane;
   In bed she moaning lay,
Till God released her from her pain,
   And then she went away.

"Master, we are Seven!"

"So in the churchyard she was laid,
And when the grass was dry,
Together around her grave we played,
My brother John and I.

"And when the ground was white with snow,
And I could run and slide,
My brother John was forced to go,
And he lies by her side."

"How many are you then," said I,
"If those two are in heaven?"
The little maiden did reply,
"Oh, master, we are seven!"

"But they are dead—those two are dead;
Their spirits are in heaven!"
'Twas throwing words away, for still
The little maid would have her will,
And said, "Nay, we are seven!"

WM. WORDSWORTH.

19

SEVEN TIMES ONE.

THERE's no dew left on the daisies and clover,
  There's no rain left in heaven;
I've said my " seven times" over and over—
  Seven times one are seven.

I am old, so old I can write a letter;
  My birth-day lessons are done;
The lambs play always, they know no better;
  They are only one times one.

O moon, in the night I've seen you sailing,
  And shining so round and low;
You were bright, ah bright, but your light is
      failing;
  You are nothing now but a bow.

You moon! have you done something wrong
      in heaven,
  That God has hidden your face?
I hope if you have, you will be forgiven,
  And shine again in your place.

O velvet bee, you're a dusty fellow;
　You've powdered your legs with gold;
O brave marshmary buds, rich and yellow,
　Give me your money to hold.

O columbine, open your folded wrapper,
　Where two twin turtle-doves dwell;
O cuckoo-pint, toll me the purple-clapper
　That hangs in your clear green bell.

And show me your nest with the young ones
　　　in it;
　I will not steal them away;
I am old, you may trust me, linnet! linnet!—
　I am seven times one to-day.

JEAN INGELOW.

ETERNITY.

How long sometimes a day appears!
　And weeks, how long are they!
Months move as slow as if the years
　Would never pass away.

Days, months and years must have an end;
　　Eternity has none;
'Twill always have as long to spend
　　As when it first begun.

Great God! although we cannot tell
　　How such a thing may be,
We humbly pray that we may dwell
　　That long, long time with thee.

　　　　　　　　　　JANE TAYLOR.

LITTLE BELL.

PIPED the blackbird on the beechwood spray,
" Little maid, slow wandering this way,
　　What's your name?" said he,
" What's your name? oh stop and straight
　　　　unfold,
Pretty maid with showery curls of gold!"
　　" Little Bell," said she.

Little Bell sat down beneath the rocks,
Tossed aside her gleamy golden locks,

"Bonny bird," said she,
"Sing me your best song before I go."
"Here's the very finest song I know,
　　Little Bell," said he.

And the blackbird piped—you never heard
Half so gay a song from any bird
　　'Neath the morning skies;
In the little childish heart below,
All its sweetness seemed to grow and grow,
And shine forth in happy overflow
　　From the bright blue eyes.

Down the dell she tripped, and through the
　　　　glade;
Peeped the squirrel from the hazel-shade,
　　And from out the tree
Swung and leaped and frolicked void of fear,
While the blackbird piped so all could hear:
　　"Little Bell," piped he.

Little Bell sat down amid the fern:
"Squirrel, squirrel, to your task return;
19 *

Bring me nuts," quoth she,
Up, away, the frisky squirrel hies—
Golden woodlights glancing in his eyes;
     And adown the tree,
Great ripe nuts, kissed brown by July sun,
In the little lap drop one by one,
Hark, how blackbird pipes to see the fun :
     " Happy Bell," pipes he.

Little Bell looked up and down the glade,
" Squirrel, squirrel, from the nut tree shade,
Bonny blackbird, if you're not afraid,
     Come and share with me."
Down came squirrel, eager for his share,
Down came bonny blackbird : I declare
Little Bell gave each his honest share ;
     Ah, the merry three !

By her snow-white cot, at close of day,
Knelt sweet Bell, with folded palms, to pray ;
     Very calm and clear
Rose the praying voice to where, unseen
In blue heaven, an angel shape serene
     Paused a while to hear.

" What good child is this," the angel said,
" That with happy heart, beside her bed,
    Prays so lovingly?"
Low and soft, oh very low and soft,
Crooned the blackbird in the orchard croft:
    " Bell, dear Bell!" crooned he.

" Whom God's creatures love," the angel fair
Murmured, " God doth bless with angels' care,
    Child, thy bed shall be
Folded safe from harm—love deep and kind
Shall watch around and leave good gifts be-
    hind,
    Little Bell, for thee."

                T. WESTWOOD.

CAT AND KITTEN.

KITTEN, kitten! two months old, woolly snow-
    ball lying snug,
Curled up in the warmest fold of the warm
    hearth-rug,
    Turn your drowsy head this way,
    What is life, O kitten, say?

Life! said the kitten, winking her eyes,
And twitching her tail in a droll surprise;
Life! Oh it's racing over the floor,
Out at the window and in at the door,
   Now on the chair-back, now on the table,
'Mid balls of cotton and skeins of silk,
And crumbs of sugar, and jugs of milk,
   All so easy and comfortable.
It's patting a little dog's ears, and leaping
Round him and over him while he's sleeping;
Waking him up in a sore affright,
Then off and away like a flash of light,
Scouring and scampering out of sight.
Life! Oh it's rolling over and over
On the summer turf and budding clover;
Chasing the shadows as fast as they run
Down the green paths in the summer sun;
Prancing and gamboling brave and bold,
Climbing the tree-stems, scratching the mould:
That's life! said the kitten, two months old!

Kitten, kitten! come sit on my knee,
And listen, kitty, listen to me!
One by one—oh one by one—
The shy, swift shadows sweep over the sun,

Daylight dieth, and kittenhood's done!
And, kitten oh the rain and the wind!
For cathood cometh, with careful mind,
And grave cat-duties follow behind ;
Hark! there's a sound you cannot hear:
I'll whisper its meaning in your ear—
  Mice!
The kitten stared with her great green eyes,
And twitched her tail in a queer surprise—
  Mice !
No more tit-bits dainty and nice,
No more mischief, and no more play,
But watching by night and sleeping by day!
Prowling wherever the foe doth lurk ;
Very short commons and very sharp work.
And, kitten, oh the hail and thunder;
That's a blackish cloud, but a blacker is under.
Hark! but you'll fall from my knee I fear,
When I whisper that awful word in your ear—
  R-r-r-r-ats ! !
The kitten's heart beat with great pit-a-pats;
But her whiskers quivered, and from their
  sheath ♭
Flashed out the sharp white, pearly teeth!

The scorn of dogs, but the terror of cats,
The cruelest foes, and the fiercest fighters,
The sauciest thieves, and the sharpest biters—
    R-r-r-r-ats !!
But, kitten, I see you've a stoutish heart,
So courage and play an honest part;
Use well your paws, and stretch out your claws,
And sharpen your teeth, and strengthen your
    jaws;
Then woe to the tribe of pickers and stealers,
Nibblers, and gnawers, and evil-dealers;
But now that you know that life's not
    precisely
The thing your fancy pictured so nicely,
Off and away, race over the floor,
Out at the window, and in at the door;
Roll on the turf, and bask in the sun,
Ere night-time cometh and kittenhood's done!

THE LITTLE FISH.

"DEAR mother!" said a little fish, "pray is
    not that a fly?
I'm very hungry and I wish you'd let me go
    and try!"

"Sweet innocent!" the mother cried, and
    started from her nook—
"That horrid fly is put to hide the sharpness
    of the hook."
Now, as I've heard, this little trout was
    young and foolish too,
And so he thought he'd venture out to see if
    it were true;
And round about the hook he played, with
    many a longing look,
And, "Dear me!" to himself he said, "I'm
    sure that's not a hook;
I can but give one little pluck; let's see, and
    so I will!"
So on he went, and lo! it stuck quite through
    his little gill;
And as he faint and fainter grew, with hol-
    low voice he cried,
"Dear mother, had I minded you, I need
    not now have died!

BETH GELERT.

THE spearman heard the bugle sound,
  And cheerily smiled the morn,
And many a dog and many a hound
  Obeyed Llewellyn's horn;
Yet still he blew a louder blast,
  And gave a lustier cheer:
"Come, Gelert, come! thou'rt never last
  Llewellyn's horn to hear."

But where does faithful Gelert roam,
  The pride of all his race—
So true, so brave, a lamb at home,
  A lion in the chase?
That day Llewellyn little loved
  The chase of hart or hare,
And scant and small the booty proved,
  For Gelert was not there.

Unpleased, Llewellyn homeward hied,
  When near his portal seat,
His truant Gelert he espied,
  Bounding his lord to meet;

But when he reached the castle door,
   Aghast the chieftain stood;
The hound was all o'er-smeared with gore;
   His lips, his fangs ran blood.

Onward in haste Llewellyn past,
   And on went Gelert too,
And still where'er his eyes he cast,
   Fresh blood-drops shocked his view;
He called his child; no voice replied;
   He searched in terror wild—
Blood, blood he found on every side,
   But nowhere found his child.

"Thou hound! my child's by thee devoured!"
   The frantic father cried,
And to the hilt his vengeful sword
   He plunged in Gelert's side;
His suppliant looks as prone he fell
   No pity could impart,
Yet still his Gelert's dying yell
   Passed heavy o'er his heart.

Aroused by Gelert's dying yell,
   Some slumberer wakened nigh;
20

What joy the parent's heart could tell
    To hear his infant cry?
No wound had he, nor harm nor dread,
    But the same couch beneath
Lay a gaunt wolf, all torn and dead,
    Tremendous still in death.

And what was then Llewellyn's pain!
    For now the truth was clear;
The gallant hound the wolf had slain
    To save Llewellyn's heir.
Vain, vain was all Llewellyn's woe:
    " Best of thy kind, adieu!
The frantic blow that laid thee low
    This heart shall ever rue."

And now a gallant tomb they raise,
    With costly sculpture decked,
And marbles storied to his praise
    Brave Gelert's bones protect.
There never yet could spearman pass
    Or forester unmoved;
And there the tear besprinkled grass
    Llewellyn's sorrow proved.

OLD BALLAD.

THE MILK-WHITE DOVE.

WILL you have a story, darling?
　I know one, very old;
For when I was a little child
　I used to hear it told.
It is about a little boy,
　And the pigeons which he sold.

His mother she was very poor,
　And kept a rich man's gate;
Until the carriages passed through,
　There Jacob had to wait.

Now Jacob was a patient lad,
　A loving, faithful son:
Of all the things the rich man had,
　He wanted only one.

A pigeon with a crested head,
　And feathers soft as silk,
With crimson feet and crimson bill,
　The rest as white as milk.

He had some pigeons of his own;
  He loved them very well;
But then his mother was so poor
  He reared them all to sell.

He kept them in a little shed
  That sloped down from the roof:
Great trouble had he every spring
  To make it waterproof.

He used to count them every day,
  To see he had them all;
They knew his footstep when he came,
  And answered to his call.

And one—a chocolate-colored hen—
  Was prettier than the rest,
Because there was a gloss like gold
  All round its throat and breast.

You know the little birds in spring
  Build houses, where they dwell,
And feed and rear their little ones,
  And love each other well.

So the black pigeons Jacob had
　　Were mated with the gray;
And crested-crown and ring-neck made
　　Their nest the first of May.

For God hath made each little bird
　　To love and need a mate;
And so the little chocolate hen
　　Was very desolate.

And Jacob thought if he could get
　　The rich man's milk-white dove,
And keep it always for his own—
　　Now, listen to me, love:

He wanted that which was not his,
　　That which another had;
And so a great temptation grew
　　Around the little lad.

The rich man had whole flocks of birds,
　　And Jacob reasoned so:
"If I should take this one white dove,
　　How can he ever know?
20 *

" Among so many can he miss
   The one which I shall take?
Among so many, many birds,
   What difference can it make?"

But, darling, even while his heart
   Throbbed with these wishes strong—
And something always troubled him—
   He knew that it was wrong.

So time passed on ; he watched the dove,
   How every day it came
Nearer and nearer to the shed,
   More gentle and more tame.

He watched it with a longing eye :
   At last, one summer day,
He saw it settle on the roof
   As if it meant to stay.

Now Jacob seemed a happy boy:
   Said he, " It has a right
To choose a dwelling anywhere
   Most pleasant in its sight."

And so he scattered grains of corn
   And crumbs of wheaten bread,
Because he thought the dove would stay
   Where it was kindly fed.

Well, time passed on—the milk-white dove,
   Well pleased with Jacob's care,
Soon learned to know him like the rest,
   And seemed right happy there.

One morning he had called them all
   Around him to be fed,
And on the ground he scattered corn,
   And peas, and crumbs of bread.

When all at once he heard a man
   Outside the road-gate call:
" Boy, if these pigeons are for sale,
   I think I'll take them all."

All! how it smote on Jacob's ear!
   " I see there are but eight:
If you will take eight shillings down,
   I'll pay you at that rate."

Now, at that moment, all the birds
    Were feeding in the sun,
But Jacob, in his startled heart,
    Could think of only one.

And never since the milk-white dove
    Had joined the chocolate hen,
Had he felt in his inmost heart
    As he was feeling then.

"Come—hurry, hurry!" said the man;
    "I have no time to lose;
Between the shillings and the birds
    It can't be hard to choose."

Poor Jacob, having once begun
    To do what was not right,
Forgetting he was standing in
    His heavenly Father's sight,

And knowing how his mother had
    A quarter's rent to pay,
Felt in his heart the sense of right
    Was fading fast away;

When from the open cottage-door
　There came a murmuring low:
It was his mother's morning hymn,
　Solemn, and sweet, and slow.

He listened, and a holy fear
　Was wakened in his heart,
And strength was given him that hour
　To choose the better part.

And turning to the stranger man
　A frank, untroubled eye,
He said : "But seven birds are mine ;
　But seven you can buy."

"Oh !" said the man, " they go in pairs,
　And will not suit me, then ;"
So Jacob sold him only six,
　And kept the chocolate hen.

And when the evening shadows came
　And dew was on the grass,
He watched outside the garden-gate
　To see the rich man pass.

And in his hand the milk-white dove
  He held with gentle care;
And many a soft caress he laid
  Upon its feathers fair.

And when at last the rich man came,
  Poor Jacob, rendered bold
By feeling he was in the right,
  His artless story told.

And after he had owned to all
  The wrong which he had done,
And the worst wrong he wished to do,
  He lifted to the sun

A happy, open, fearless face,
  Which won the rich man's love;
And so he bade him always keep
  For his the milk-white dove.

And Jacob, once more good and true,
  Stood in his mother's sight,
The struggle of temptation past,
  The wrong all turned to right.

And Jacob, with a heart at rest,
    Lay down upon his bed;
And whiter wings than his white dove's
    Were round his pillow spread.

NOT READY FOR SCHOOL.

PRAY, where is my hat—it is taken away,
    And my shoe-strings are all in a knot;
I can't find a thing where it should be to-
    day,
    Though I've hunted in every spot.

Do, Rachel, just look for my Atlas up stairs,
    My Æsop is somewhere there too;
And, sister, just brush down these trouble-
    some hairs,
    And, mother, just fasten my shoe.

And, sister, beg father to write an excuse,
    But stop; he will only say " No,"
And go on with a smile, and keep reading
    the news,
    While everything bothers me so.

My satchel is heavy and ready to fall;
　　This old pop-gun is breaking my map;
I'll have nothing to do with pop-gun or ball,
　　There's no playing for such a poor chap.

The town-clock will strike in a minute, I fear,
　　Then away to the foot I must sink;
There! look at my Carpenter tumbled down
　　　　here,
　　And my Worcester covered with ink.

I wish I'd not lingered at breakfast the last,
　　Though the toast and the butter were fine;
I think that our Edward must eat pretty fast,
　　To be off when I haven't done mine.

Now Edward and Henry protest they won't
　　　　wait,
　　And beat on the door with their sticks;
I suppose they will say I was dressing too late;
　　To-morrow I'll be up at six.
　　　　　　　　　　　　Mrs. Gilman.

INDEX OF SUBJECTS.

	PAGE
A CHILD's Dream of Heaven	125
A Lost Day	106
An English Child in the Days of Wickliffe	77
Anna's Good Resolutions	18
Bessie Bell	45
Beth Gelert	228
Bird's Nest	208
Bob-o'-Link	187
Busy Bee	39
Cat and Kitten	223
Christ and the Little Ones	27
Cradle Hymn	35
Cradle Hymn	42
Eternity	219
Evening Hymn	40
Evening Hymn	57
Evening Prayer	21
Forgiving	16

PAGE

God Sees Me.. 10
Good-morning 192
Good-night and Good-morning................. 52

Katie's Dream.. 66

Let it Pass.................................... 60
Little Bell 220
Little Bessie...... 107
Little Deeds.. 50
Little Dick Snappy 13
Little Mary.. 21
Little People...................................... 5
Little Things.................................... 34
Little Willie and the Apple......... 104

Mary Dow.. 178
Minutes and Years... 205
Morning Hymn.. 20
Mother's Last Words... 128
Mrs. Lofty and I.. 59
My Little Lammie 175
My Little Sister........... 204
My Mother.. 28

Not Ready for School... 239

On the Lord's Side.. 22
Our Baby.. 47

PAGE

Our Father 36

" Paddle your own Canoe" 12
" Patchie" 64
Poor Mamma 190
Popping Corn 19
Pride and Humility 56
Pussy-Cat 210

Ready for Duty 122
Ringing the Bell 119
Robin Redbreast 23
Robins 58

Seven Times One 218
Shadows 62
Speak Gently 54

The Baby 41
The Bath 209

The Blackberry-Girl 97
The Blessing of Labor 53
The Blind Boy 114
The Boy and the Flowers 26
The Boy who Never tells a Lie 182
The Childhood of Jesus 118
The Children's Hymn 31
The Child's First Grief 55

PAGE

The Commandments... 31
The Drummer-Boy's Burial.................... 183
The Father of the Fatherless.................................... 101
The Grain of Corn and the Penny........................... 49
The Gray Swan........ 211
The Heavenly Father..... 116
The Little Angel........ 121
The Little Doves.. 173
The Little Fish............................... 226
The Little Match-Girl.. 89
The Lost Child... 85
The Love of Christ............... 33
The Milk-white Dove... 231
The Patter of Little Feet 7
The Snow-Bird.. 198
The Spider and the Fly.. 194
The Squirrel.. 180
The Stolen Nest.. 200
The Strange Child's Christmas....'...................... 110
The Sweet Story 32
The Tempest at Sea.............................. 84
The Two Pennies... 37
The Wood-Mouse... 74
To-day and To-morrow.. 43
Touch Not, Taste Not.. 57
Treasure on Earth and Treasure in Heaven.................. 11
Tumble... 205
Twinkle, Little Star... 38
Two Little Robins.. 48

PAGE

Vesper............ 40

We are Seven.. 214
What I Hate... 206
What I Love... 207
Who shall Stand in the Holy Place?........................... 169
Wonderful Night !.. 24
Work and Play.. 44

21 *

INDEX OF FIRST LINES.

	PAGE
A DEAR little girl sat under a tree	52
A dreary place would be this earth	5
A grain of corn an infant's hand	49
A little bird built a warm nest in a tree	208
A little child, she read a book beside an open door	77
All day long the storm of battle	183
Alone, beneath the heavy shade	85
A missionary far away	119
Another little wave upon the sea of life	41
A penny I have, it is all my own	37
As I walked over the hills one day	175
A squirrel sat on the topmost limb	180
A very pretty sight this morning I did see	58
Before the bright sun rises over the hill	21
Ben Adam had a golden coin one day	11
Be not swift to take offence—let it pass!	60
Call that day lost whose setting sun	106
Come here, little Robin, and don't be afraid	23
Come in, little stranger, I said	178

PAGE

Daffy-down-dilly came up in the cold...................... 122
Dearest Father! dwelling high............................ 36
Dearest mother, get my bonnet, do!...................... 190
Dear mother, I dreamed about heaven........ 125
"Dear mother!" said a little fish, "pray is not that a
    fly?".. 226
Dear mother, why do all the girls...................... 45
Do you know the little wood-mouse?...................... 72

God's trumpet wakes the slumbering world................ 22
Glory to thee, my God, this night...................... 40

High on the top of an old pine tree.................... 173
How doth the little busy bee........ 39
How long sometimes a day appears!..................... 219
How proud we are, how fond of show!.................. 56
Hug me closer, closer, mother........................ 107
Hush, my dear; lie still and slumber................. 35

I hate to see a little girl who does not love to rise... 206
I have a little sister; she's only two years old............ 204
I knew a widow very poor............................ 101
I love the good splashing and plunging and dashing.... 209
I love to see a little girl rise with the lark so bright...... 207
I met a little cottage girl.......................... 214
In the green fields of Palestine..................... 118
I think, when I read that sweet story of old............. 32
It was a blessed summer's day...................... 114
It was a warm and sultry afternoon................... 66

PAGE

Jesus loves me—this I know............................. 33
Jesus, tender Shepherd, hear me........................ 57

Kitten, kitten! two months old, woolly snowball lying
   snug.. 223

Labor gives rest from the sorrows that greet us........... 53
Little Dick Snappy was always unhappy.................... 13
Little drops of water, little grains of sand............... 34
Little Willie stood under an apple tree old............... 104
Little Gretchen, little Gretchen........................ 89

Merrily swinging on brier and weed...................... 187
Mrs. Lofty keeps a carriage—so do I..................... 57

Not mighty deeds make up the sum of happiness below. 50
Now I lay me down to sleep............................. 21

Oh call my brother back to me.......................... 55
"Oh I am so happy!" a little girl said.................. 192
Oh tell me, sailor, tell me true....................... 211
Oh who before the righteous God........................ 169
Once there was a little boy............................ 182
One autumn night, when the wind was high............... 19

Piped the blackbird on the beechwood spray............. 220
Pray, where is my hat—it is taken away................. 239
Pussy-cat lives in the servants' hall.................. 210

Right into our house one day........................... 121

	PAGE
Sing to the Lord the children's hymn	31
Sixty seconds make one minute	205
Speak gently: it is better far	54
Sweet baby, sleep? what ails my dear?	42
The bell had rung, the school was out	64
The candles are lighted, the fire blazes bright	62
The ground was all covered with snow one day	198
"The Master has come over Jordan"	72
The morning bright with rosy light	20
There's no dew left on the daisies and clover	218
There went a stranger child	110
The spearman heard the bugle sound	228
The yellow fog lay thick and dim	128
This is the just and great command	31
Thou that rulest earth and heaven	40
Through all the busy daylight, through all the quiet night	10
To-day! a lisping child, with hair all golden.	43
To-day we cut the fragrant sod with trembling hands asunder	47
Touch not the tempting cup, my boy, though urged by friend or foe	57
To-whit, to-whit, to-whee! will you listen to me?	200
Tumble up, tumble down, never mind it, my sweet!	205
Twinkle, twinkle, little star	38
Two Robin Redbreasts built their nest	48
Up this world and down this world	12
Up with the sun in the morning	7

PAGE

Well, now I'll sit down and I'll work very fast..... 18

We were crowded in the cabin................................. 84

When thou art kneeling down at night.......... ...., 16

Who fed me from her gentle breast.......... 28

Why, Phœbe, are you come so soon ?......................... 95

Willie, with a spirit light, was a happy little child....... 26

Will you have a story, darling ?............................... 231

"Will you walk into my parlor?" said the spider to

the fly... 194

Within a town of Holland once............................... 116

Wonderful night.. 24

Work while you work, play while you play................. 44